Professional Careers Series

 **CAREERS** in

TRAVEL, TOURISM & HOSPITALITY

MARJORIE EBERTS, LINDA BROTHERS, ANN GISLER

SECOND EDITION

McGraw·Hill

New York   Chicago   San Francisco   Lisbon   London   Madrid   Mexico City
Milan   New Delhi   San Juan   Seoul   Singapore   Sydney   Toronto

Library of Congress Cataloging-in-Publication Data

Eberts, Marjorie.
    Careers in travel, tourism & hospitality / by Marjorie Eberts, Linda Brothers, Ann Gisler.—
2nd ed.
        p.   cm. — (McGraw-Hill professional careers series)
    Rev. ed of : Careers in travel, tourism, and hospitality. c1997.
    ISBN 0-07-144856-X (alk. paper)
        1. Tourism—Vocational guidance.   I. Title : Careers in travel, tourism, and hospitality.
II. Brothers, Linda.   III. Gisler, Ann.   IV. Eberts, Marjorie. Careers in travel, tourism, and
hospitality.   V. Title.

G155.5.E24   2006
910'.23—dc22   2005005482

To the Eberts, Brothers, and Gisler families, with whom
the authors have shared so many delightful travel, tourism,
and hospitality experiences

2 3 4 5 6 7 8 9 0   DOC/DOC   0 9 8 7 6

ISBN 0-07-144856-X

This book is printed on acid-free paper.

CONTENTS

CHAPTER 13

Careers at Hotels, Motels, and Other Lodgings   123

Settings for lodgings • Looking at lodging jobs by department • Looking at a job as a front desk clerk • Working conditions • Preparation for becoming a front desk clerk • Special attributes of front desk clerks • Advancement • Salary and benefits • The personal story of a front desk clerk • Looking at a career as a manager • Working conditions • Preparation for becoming a manager • Special attributes of managers • Advancement • Salary and benefits • The personal story of a general manager • The personal story of a sales manager • The personal story of a food and beverage director • The personal story of an executive housekeeper • The future • For more information

CHAPTER 14

Career Opportunities in Restaurants   139

Looking at jobs in restaurants • Looking at jobs in sit-down restaurants • Looking at a career as a restaurant manager • Working conditions • Preparation for becoming a restaurant manager • Salary, benefits, and advancement • The personal story of a restaurant manager • The future for restaurant managers • Preparation for owning a restaurant • The personal story of two restaurant owners • Looking at the jobs of chefs, cooks, and other kitchen employees • Responsibilities by department • Working conditions • Preparation for becoming a chef, cook, or kitchen employee • Special attributes of chefs, cooks, or kitchen employees • Advancement • Salary and benefits • The personal story of a chef • The future for chefs, cooks, and kitchen employees • Looking at jobs in fast-food restaurants • Looking at a job as an hourly employee • Preparation for becoming an hourly employee • Advancement • Salary and benefits • The personal story of an hourly employee • Looking at a career as a fast-food restaurant manager • Working conditions • Preparation for becoming a fast-food restaurant manager • Advancement • Salary and benefits • The personal story of a fast-food restaurant manager • The future of the fast-food industry • For more information

AN OVERVIEW OF CAREERS IN TRAVEL, TOURISM, AND HOSPITALITY

The tourism industry in the United States is the first, second-, or third-largest employer in thirty of the fifty states, which adds up to millions of career opportunities with airlines; hotels and motels; restaurants; cruise lines; travel agencies; tour operators; amusement parks; tourist attractions; and national, state, and local parks. Unfortunately, employment in tourism tumbled from the peak year of 2000 due to a weak economy and security concerns. Since 2004, however, employment has rebounded, and most industry experts believe that trend will continue. People are once again taking cruises, joining tour groups, eating in restaurants, and staying in hotels.

TRAVEL, TOURISM, AND HOSPITALITY

Selecting a career in travel, tourism, and hospitality is rewarding because these careers involve helping others have a good time. These careers also give people opportunities to work with or play host to just about everyone. Movie stars and sports heroes fly on planes, eat in restaurants, stay at hotels, and visit tourist attractions. So do ordinary citizens, politicians, foreign dignitaries, and affluent business executives.

While experience and education determine where people start in these careers, there is no limit to where their talents and ambition can take them. One of the great appeals of careers in travel, tourism, and hospitality is the opportunity for motivated people of all ages and backgrounds to move up the career ladder rapidly or even to own their own business. For example, Julie and Bill Brice managed a frozen yogurt stand in their late teens. When the owner put their unit and the one he managed up for sale, they bought both units with the $10,000 they had saved for college, and the I Can't Believe It's Yogurt chain was founded.

Lack of experience is no barrier to employment or advancement in many travel, tourism, and hospitality careers. Many of today's fast-food company executives started out as hourly workers. John Hyduke, vice president of franchise development at Dairy Queen, started out working in the store owned and operated by his parents.

Of course, some careers in travel, tourism, and hospitality, such as pilot, flight attendant, travel agent, and chef, require specialized training. Specialized training and education beyond high school can also help individuals get ahead faster. Many two- and four-year colleges, universities, and vocational/technical schools have hospitality and tourism programs that prepare people to move into management positions.

The three career areas of travel, tourism, and hospitality provide many other special opportunities. Individuals choosing careers in these areas can stay in their own community or explore fascinating locations around the world. They can set up a health club in a hotel in Africa or one next to a hometown airport; cook in Paris, France, or Paris, Kentucky; or lead tours to South America or to local historic spots.

Careers in travel, tourism, and hospitality can be found in a variety of enterprises:

adventure travel companies	publishing houses
airlines	railroad and bus companies
amusement parks	riverboats
camps	sit-down and fast-food
cruise ships	restaurants
hotels and motels	tour companies
national, state, and local	tourist attractions
parks	travel agencies

These opportunities are described in more detail throughout this book.

LEARNING ABOUT CAREERS IN TRAVEL, TOURISM, AND HOSPITALITY

The best way to become acquainted with the opportunities in these career areas is by taking a part-time job. Working the actual job demonstrates what so many opportunities, from hotels to amusement parks to local parks, are really like. And it also lets individuals assess both whether they would enjoy this career and whether it is appropriate for them.

Another great way to learn about any career in travel, tourism, and hospitality is to research what has been written in books and online. Websites of associations for particular careers offer many insights and tips about each field. The *Occupational Outlook Handbook*, compiled by the United States Department of Labor, also has information on most careers from chef to pilot to forest ranger. The handbook contains information about working conditions, employment opportunities, training required, advancement opportunities, earnings, and future job outlook. Throughout this book, the "For More Information" sections list helpful sources, especially websites, for even more career information.

C H A P T E R

CAREERS AS A TRAVEL AGENT

Travel agents spend their days helping tourists realize personal dreams of travel throughout the world and helping businesspeople reach their destinations. It is a very satisfying career for those who love to be involved with travel every day, to do research, to handle thousands of details, to talk with people, and to spend a lot of time on the computer. Another big dividend of this profession is the travel perks agents receive, including the opportunity to travel free or at reduced rates to places in the United States and around the world.

TRAVEL AGENCIES

Thomas Cook is often called the father of the travel agency industry. He organized his first tour in 1841, and his company is still serving travelers throughout the world. Cook established the way most travel agencies would operate. He did not charge customers for his travel services, instead receiving commissions from rail companies on each ticket he sold. Most travel agencies still derive their income primarily from commissions paid by hotels, resorts, cruise lines, rental car companies, and other enterprises with which they make reservations for clients.

Today, there are more than twenty-two thousand travel agencies in the United States. Some of these agencies are parts of large chains like American Express and Carlson Wagonlit Travel, but more are independent operators. Nearly 50 percent of the travel agencies are located in suburban areas, about 40 percent are in large cities, and the rest are in small towns and rural areas. Travel agencies employ more than one hundred thousand travel agents. Most travel agencies are small, with fewer than ten employees.

According to the American Society of Travel Agents (ASTA), the largest and most influential travel trade association, the majority of travel agencies specialize in certain services or destinations. One important aspect of specialization concerns the type of clientele that a travel agency serves. Corporate, or commercial, agencies cater predominantly, or perhaps exclusively, to the travel needs of business travelers. This type of agency actively seeks new corporate accounts and may contract with companies to be their travel arranger. Vacation, or leisure, agencies, on the other hand, assist individuals or groups in making vacation or other leisure travel plans. Many individual travel agents have specialized skills and work exclusively as either corporate or leisure agents. Of course, there are also travel agencies that provide services for both business- and vacation-oriented travelers.

LOOKING AT A CAREER AS A TRAVEL AGENT

Americans now make over one billion trips a year. The average traveler is confronted with many alternatives for transportation, accommodations, and other travel services. Today's travel agents give travelers advice on destinations and make arrangements for transportation, hotel accommodations, tours, car rentals, and recreation. They may also advise on weather conditions, restaurants, and tourist attractions and recreation as well as sell travel insurance. For international travel, agents also provide information on customs regulations, required papers (passports, visas, and certificates of vaccination), and currency exchange rates. Travel agents who plan conventions and other meetings are usually called meeting planners (see Chapter 12).

Most travel agents work at agencies and sell travel arrangements directly to clients. Besides business or leisure travel, they may specialize in an area such as cruises or adventure travel. Travel agents can also work for corporations, arranging travel for employees and clients; for universities that have travel programs for students and alumni; for membership organizations or associations offering travel programs for members; and for banks with travel departments. Many agents are self-employed.

WORKING CONDITIONS

Travel agencies are located everywhere from stand-alone offices to department stores to skyscrapers. Typically, all of the agents work in one large room; however, in larger agencies, managers may have private offices. Quite often, the room is noisy, with phones ringing, keyboards clicking, printers operating, and clients and agents holding conversations. With the emergence of advanced computer systems and telecommunication networks, some travel agents are able to work at home.

Travel agents tend to work forty-hour weeks and frequently work on Saturdays. Work hours are dictated by the clients' needs. If the clientele consists solely of businesspeople, work hours will mirror the typical business week. If most clients are making personal travel plans, then the agency is likely to be open later in the evening and on Saturdays. No matter where a travel agent works, it will often be necessary to work longer hours during vacation seasons and/or periods of heavy business travel to finalize travel plans and to get tickets to customers. Agents who are self-employed usually work longer hours.

RESPONSIBILITIES

Beginning travel agents may not have all of the responsibilities of more experienced agents. They may spend more time greeting customers and directing them to other agents, handling routine office mail, filing brochures, and handling simple travel requests. They may also assist experienced agents in expediting complicated orders.

Making Arrangements

The major responsibilities of travel agents are to handle requests for information and to make travel arrangements. Their clients will either come into their office or call on the phone.

Promoting Sales

People may not realize that part of the job of being a travel agent is promoting sales. To be successful, an agency must have both repeat clients and new clients. Handling a client's travel needs successfully can lead to that client not only coming back to the agency but referring his or her friends there, too. It can also lead to securing corporate accounts. Travel agents find additional clients by approaching groups such as fraternal, religious, or social organizations and offering to put together a vacation package that can be sold only to the membership. One way for agents to court business travelers is by contacting corporations and describing their services. By getting to know meeting planners, travel agents can find opportunities to make travel arrangements for these professionals.

PREPARATION FOR BECOMING A TRAVEL AGENT

Formal or specialized training is becoming increasingly important for travel agents, because few agencies are willing to train people on the job. Consider for a moment some of the many things a travel agent is expected to know, from air travel regulations to government paperwork for visas and passports and from ticketing procedures to world geography, and it becomes clear how important this training is.

Training Opportunities

Many vocational schools offer full-time travel agent programs that last for several months or that take place during evenings and weekends. Travel agent courses can also be found in public adult education programs and in community and four-year colleges. A few colleges offer a bachelor's degree and a master's degree in travel and tourism. Although few college courses relate directly to the travel industry, a college education is sometimes desired by employers. Courses in computer science, geography, foreign languages, and history are most useful. Courses in accounting and business management also are important, especially for those who expect to manage or start their own travel agencies. Travel agencies also provide some on-the-job training for their employees, a significant part of which consists of computer instruction. Agents must have computer skills to operate airline reservations systems.

Choosing a Travel School

Travel agents clearly need certain skills and knowledge. Attending a school to help acquire these skills should make prospective agents more marketable. ASTA suggests that individuals ask the following questions of the representatives of the educational institutions that they are considering attending.

• Has the school been approved, registered, or licensed by the state postsecondary education bureau or a recognized accreditation association? If the school's catalog or brochure shows no indication of some sort of accreditation, check with the state department of education in the state where the school is located. For additional information, contact the Better Business Bureau in the city or town where the school is located.

• Who teaches on the faculty? How many members of the faculty have recent travel industry experience or certified travel counselor (CTC) designation? Are they professionally active within the travel and tourism industry?

• What does the curriculum offer? Does it offer travel courses in geography, fares/ticketing/tariffs, industry forms and procedures, automation, sales, marketing, and travel industry operations? Does the school provide for internships? Does the school offer extracurricular activities? Is the course of study of sufficient duration to cover adequately the curriculum advertised?

• What kind of hands-on airline computer training is available? Does it teach both domestic and international reservations? Does the training cover accessing airline availability, pricing, selling, and creating a passenger name record (PNR) as well as booking hotel, car rental, and rail reservations?

• How long has the school been in operation? Is the school a member of ASTA? Does the school have a good relationship with the local travel agency community? Does the school have an advisory board of active travel industry professionals?

• Does the school offer placement assistance for graduates? If so, what is its success ratio? Feel free to ask if any graduates of the school are working in the area and if you can contact them. Ask working graduates for their evaluation of the program.

Certification, Licensing, and Advancement

The first level of certification of the Travel Institute is the Certified Travel Associate (CTA) program. It is designed for travel agents in the early stages of their careers. It covers five core skills areas: communication, technology, geography, sales and service, and travel industry. To get this certification, travel agents must possess eighteen months of industry experience and complete testing. To keep the certification, they must earn ten continuing units each year.

Travel agents with five or more years of experience who have CTA certification can take an advanced course leading to the designation of Certified Travel Counselor (CTC). This certification is the hallmark of a truly professional agent. Owners and managers of agencies tend to have this certification. The Institute of Certified Travel Agents also offers courses leading to certification, called designation of competence, in North American, western European, Caribbean, or South Pacific tours. This certification indicates that an agent has an in-depth knowledge of one or more of these travel areas.

There are no federal licensing requirements for travel agents. However, certain states require licensing, and several have registration requirements.

Some employees start as reservation clerks or receptionists in travel agencies. With experience and some formal training, they take on greater responsibilities and eventually assume travel agent duties. In agencies with many offices, travel agents may advance to office manager or to other managerial positions. Many agents advance up the career ladder by moving from one agency to another. In all cases, the key to advancement is a demonstrated ability to attract new clients and to do work at such a level that most clients become repeat clients.

Travel agents who start their own agencies usually have experience in an established agency first. They must generally gain formal approval from suppliers or corporations—organizations of airlines, ship lines, or rail lines—before they can receive commissions. The Airlines Reporting Corporation, for example, is the approving body for airlines. To gain approval, an agency must be in operation, be financially sound, and employ at least one experienced manager or travel agent.

Continuing Education

No one should become a travel agent without being willing to learn continually throughout his or her career. Change is a constant in this profession. Agencies change the computer programs they use. New databases are constantly being added to computer systems. Tour companies and cruise lines offer new tours each year. And airline rates may change almost daily, even to the same destination. New hotels are built throughout the world, and tourist "hot spots" change. Travel agents keep up-to-date on their profession by reading professional publications and taking courses offered by the Institute of Certified Travel Agents and the American Society of Travel Agents. These courses allow them to expand their knowledge of such areas as mature, family, and niche travel and newer destinations such as Cuba and Bhutan as well as how to improve their sales and marketing skills.

SPECIAL ATTRIBUTES OF TRAVEL AGENTS

Travel agents are salespeople. And to be successful in this facet of their jobs, they must be able to get along with clients and handle complaints. They should be engaging and enthusiastic as well as both patient and persistent. They need to know how to discover what clients really want, have a thorough knowledge of the options available, and then be able to close a sale. No one is born with a sales personality. These are skills that can be developed.

Every year, more sophisticated computer systems are used in the travel industry. Travel agents must be sufficiently skilled in using these systems to access air, rail, cruise, tour, and accommodations information and to book reservations. In addition, agents must know how to prioritize their work so that clients receive tickets and information when needed. Some ticketing must be done immediately, while other ticketing can be postponed.

SALARY AND BENEFITS

Future travel agents need to understand that agencies now earn their income from commissions and client fees. Just a few years ago, travel agencies earned their income primarily from commissions. In 2002, however, the air carriers in the United States stopped paying base commissions to travel agents. While agencies still earn commissions from hotels, cruise lines, travel suppliers, and tour operators, 95 percent of all agencies now charge service fees. These fees are charged for all airline-related work and may also be charged for trip research, Amtrak, car rental, and hotel-only reservations.

Agencies have what are known as inside sales agents, outside sales agents, or both inside and outside sales agents. Outside agents may rent a desk at an agency and typically work on fees and commissions. Inside agents are hourly employees who usually do not receive commissions.

According to the Bureau of Labor Statistics, the average annual salary of a travel agent is close to $30,000 a year. Beginning agents may earn less than $20,000, while experienced agents can earn more than $40,000 annually. Travel agents' salaries depend on experience, seniority, and the size and location of the firm. Agencies focusing on corporate sales typically pay higher salaries and provide more extensive benefits than those focusing on leisure travel. Benefits may include medical insurance plans, sick leave, paid holidays and vacation days, and familiarization trips. And according to ASTA, one travel agency in five offers its employees a retirement plan. In addition, good salespeople can earn bonuses or free or discounted trips.

Earnings of travel agents who own their agencies depend mainly on commissions from travel-related bookings and the service fees they charge clients. Often it takes time for them to acquire a sufficient number of clients to have adequate earnings. And even established agents have lower profits during economic downturns.

PERKS AND PRESSURES OF BEING A TRAVEL AGENT

The major perk of being a travel agent is reduced-rate or, occasionally, free travel. Familiarization, or "fam," trips are sponsored by airlines, tour operators, and even governments to acquaint agents with a specific region. They involve visits to a great number of hotels, restaurants, and tourist attractions and are not vacations. These trips generally require agents to pay a small amount and rarely include travel companions. Airlines do give free and discounted tickets to a limited number of agents. This represents an enormous saving on international travel because the agent's ticket cost is often discounted 75 percent and a companion's fare up to 50 percent. Tours and hotels also offer discounts; however, they are frequently only 10 percent off the established price.

Although the travel perks can be impressive, there are downsides to this career. Prospective travel agents must realize that they will be spending a great portion of their day at a computer, which can cause wrist injuries and eye and back strain. The rapid work pace in many agencies and many factors beyond agents' control, such as cancelled flights, overbooked hotels, and tour destination changes, also cause stress. And there is the continual challenge of dealing with demanding and difficult clients.

THE PERSONAL STORY OF A TRAVEL AGENT

Sylvia Porter has been a travel agent for more than eight years. After graduating from college with a bachelor's degree in English, Sylvia trained teachers from throughout the world to operate the Opticon, a device that allows the blind to read by feeling print. This job, which involved some travel in the United States as well as a trip abroad to Greece, instilled in Sylvia a desire to travel and to have a career that involved travel.

Sylvia enrolled in a community college and received a degree in tourism. She explains that this training is absolutely necessary because it teaches prospective travel agents how to use the computer in a travel agency and how to research destination information.

Sylvia's first position was in a small travel agency with three inside agents. Sylvia primarily handled leisure clients, selling tours and creating foreign travel packages for those who wanted to travel independently. As an inside agent, she handled clients who walked in the door and at the same time tried to build a client base of repeat customers. She received an hourly salary and no commission.

In her next job, Sylvia became an outside agent. Her income was now based solely on the commissions she earned, and she had to attract her own clients. At this agency, she spent most of her time helping clients make leisure travel plans, although she did have some corporate accounts. As an outside agent, Sylvia was able to make more money than she did in her previous job as an inside agent.

Sylvia's current job is also as an outside agent. Although she works independently, she and four of the other agents in the firm cover for each other so that all are able to take vacations and still serve their clients. In this job, she splits her commission and fees with the agency.

Every day, she spends a lot of time on the phone with clients, considerable time on the computer, and some time with clients who come into the office. On a typical day, Sylvia might do tasks ranging from planning a trip for an independent tour in Alaska to researching Panama Canal cruise ships. Recently, Sylvia and her husband took a free cruise in exchange for doing hospitality work. They only had to pay their airfare. On the negative side, Sylvia is disappointed with the low pay agents earn for doing so much work.

THE FUTURE

The number of travel agents has remained fairly steady in recent years despite an economic downturn and safety concerns. More people are going online to book their own travel on the Internet, which reduces the number of travel agents needed. However, this decline is moderated by projections for increased spending on tourism and travel over the next decade. More people are expected to travel on vacation and to do so more frequently than in the past. Business travel is bouncing back as business activity expands in the United States and as more businesses open offices and sell products throughout the world. Furthermore, agencies are now offering tours for the growing number of foreign visitors. Many job openings will arise as new agencies start up and existing agencies expand to meet the needs of these additional travelers, but most will occur as experienced agents transfer to other occupations or leave the workforce.

The travel industry generally is sensitive to economic downturns and political crises, when travel plans are likely to be deferred. Therefore, the number of job opportunities fluctuates. The best opportunities will be for those travel agents who can utilize the Internet for their own operations to reduce costs and better compete with travel suppliers.

FOR MORE INFORMATION

A list of schools that offer training for becoming a travel agent appears in Appendix A. Individuals who are thinking about a career as a travel agent need to become acquainted with the American Society of Travel Agents for information about becoming a travel agent and what is happening in the industry. Prospective travel agents also need to become acquainted with the Travel Institute to learn more about certification and training opportunities. These two organizations offer a wealth of career information.

American Society of Travel Agents (ASTA)
Education Department
1101 King Street, Suite 200
Alexandria, VA 22314
astanet.com

The Travel Institute
145 Linden Street, Suite 305
Wellesley, MA 02482
thetravelinstitute.com

CHAPTER 3

CAREERS AS A PILOT OR FLIGHT ATTENDANT

Air travel is likely to touch the lives of most people in this country for leisure or business trips. Each year, more than two billion people throughout the world take to the air. To help them accomplish this dream, several hundred thousand workers both in the air and on the ground have exciting careers in the airline industry.

LOOKING AT A CAREER AS A PILOT

Pilots are highly trained professionals who fly airplanes and helicopters. The vast majority of pilots work for airlines transporting passengers and cargo. Others are involved in more unusual tasks, such as testing aircraft, monitoring traffic, rescuing and evacuating injured persons, firefighting, and crop dusting.

There are three positions for professional pilots in the cockpit. The captain commands the aircraft, supervises all of the other crew members, and is responsible for the safety of the passengers, crew, and cargo. The copilot, or first officer, assists the captain in communicating with air traffic controllers, monitoring the instruments, and flying the aircraft. The flight engineer, or second officer, assists the other pilots by monitoring and operating many of the instruments and systems, making minor in-flight repairs, and watching for other aircraft. Being a flight engineer does not necessarily include flying the airplane. While some large aircraft still have a flight engineer in the cockpit, virtually all new aircraft now fly with only two pilots, who rely more heavily on computerized controls.

WORKING CONDITIONS

By federal law, airline pilots cannot fly more than one hundred hours a month or one thousand hours a year. Most airline pilots fly an average of seventy-five hours a month and work an additional seventy-five hours a month performing nonflying duties before and after flights. As airlines operate flights at all hours of the day and night, pilots can expect irregular hours. They can also expect layovers away from home. During these layovers, they receive hotel accommodations, transportation between the hotel and airport, and an allowance for expenses.

Pilots employed outside the passenger airlines often have irregular schedules; they may fly as few as thirty hours one month and as many as one hundred hours the next. For example, corporate pilots do not usually fly scheduled routes. Instead, they are on call most of the month and fly when businesspeople schedule trips. Because these pilots are transporting corporate employees, they are usually home each evening and rarely fly on holidays. They will frequently have many nonflying responsibilities and much less free time than airline pilots.

RESPONSIBILITIES

Commercial airline pilots must arrive at the airport a set amount of time before each flight. After checking in, pilots typically receive information regarding weather, routing, winds, fuel load, and the optimal runway and takeoff speed. Based on this information, they choose a route, altitude, and speed that should provide the fastest, safest, and smoothest flight.

Once aboard the aircraft, pilots use a checklist to thoroughly check that the engines, controls, instruments, and other systems of the aircraft are functioning properly. They also make sure that the baggage or cargo has been loaded correctly, and they brief flight attendants about the trip.

Takeoff and landing are the most difficult parts of the flight, requiring close coordination between the captain and copilot and, if aboard, the flight engineer. During the flight, the captain pilots the aircraft along the prede-termined route with the assistance of autopilot and the flight management computer. The pilots periodically scan the instrument panel to check their fuel supply; the condition of their engines; and the air-conditioning, hydraulic, and other systems. The position of the plane is monitored by air traffic control radar stations along the way. During the flight, the pilots may request a change in altitude or route if the circumstances, such as turbu-lence, warrant it. Once on the ground, pilots must complete records on the flight for their airlines and the Federal Aviation Administration (FAA).

The number of nonflying duties that pilots have depends on where they are employed. Airline pilots have the services of large support staffs; how-ever, pilots employed by other organizations such as charters or corporate operators have many other duties. They may load the aircraft, handle all passenger luggage to ensure a balanced load, and supervise refueling. Other nonflying responsibilities include keeping records, scheduling flights, arranging for major maintenance, and even performing minor maintenance and repair work on aircraft.

PREPARATION FOR BECOMING A PILOT

Whether they are employed by major airlines, commuter airlines, corpo-rations, or cargo airlines, all pilots must meet very specific requirements. The FAA sets the standards for pilots and other people working in the avi-ation field.

Experience Requirements

For pilots, experience is judged in two ways: hours of flying and kind of flying. Certain levels must be reached in both categories for an individual to qualify for any of the basic pilot certificates issued by the FAA. For exam-ple, helicopter pilots must have at least 250 hours of flight time and an instrument rating, and airline pilots need a minimum of 1,500 hours of fly-ing experience, preferably in multiengine turbine aircraft. Most applicants exceed the minimum experience requirements. According to the Airline Pilots Association, the average new hire at regional airlines has over 2,000 hours; the average new hire at a major airline has almost 4,000.

Personal Requirements

The FAA has set a minimum age of eighteen for commercial pilots and twenty-three for air transport pilots. There is also a maximum age of sixty for commercial airline pilots. To earn a pilot's certificate, applicants must meet very stringent physical requirements, which include having 20/20 vision with or without correction, good hearing, good health, and no physical handicaps that could impair their performance. Furthermore, pilots must pass periodic medical examinations to maintain a valid certificate. Prospective pilots should have a physical examination by an FAA-designated aviation medical examiner to make sure they meet the physical requirements for a pilot's certificate before beginning a formal training program. Pilots must also demonstrate to airline companies that they can make quick decisions and accurate judgments under pressure by passing required psychological and aptitude tests.

Educational Requirements

Some small airlines hire high school graduates. While larger airlines require two years of college, more than 90 percent of the pilots with major airlines have four-year college degrees. Furthermore, airlines prefer to hire college graduates. College graduates may choose to major in aviation; however, airlines do not specify a particular major.

License Requirements

To qualify for one of the four main types of pilot certificates (student, private, commercial, air transport pilot), applicants must meet age, physical, education, and skill level requirements set by the FAA. Applicants must pass a written test that includes questions on the principles of safe flight, navigation techniques, and FAA regulations. They also must demonstrate their flying ability to FAA or designated examiners.

All categories of licenses require that pilots have recent experience and that they take a flight review with an instructor at least every two years. In addition to taking regular six-month or annual FAA and company flight checks and simulator and medical exams, pilots are subject to unannounced spot checks by FAA inspectors.

Company Requirements

Besides specific FAA requirements, pilots who want to work for airlines must also meet the individual requirements of the airlines. Successful job candidates typically have more education, ratings, and flight hours than the minimum requirements.

Training Opportunities

Many pilots are trained in the armed forces. Military pilots get extensive flying experience on jet aircraft and helicopters. At the end of their tours of duty, many pilots leave the military for civilian jobs. Because of budget reductions, it is expected that fewer pilots will be able to receive military training in the future and that more pilots will receive their training at FAA-certified schools. At the present time, the FAA has certified about six hundred civilian flying schools, including some colleges and universities that offer degree credit for pilot training.

ADVANCEMENT

New airline pilots usually start as copilots. Many begin with smaller regional or commuter airlines where they gain experience. These jobs often lead to higher paying jobs with bigger national airlines. At organizations other than airlines, new employees usually start as copilots or fly less-sophisticated equipment. Helicopter pilots typically start by flying single-engine aircraft.

Advancement for all pilots generally is limited to other flying jobs. In the airlines, advancement usually depends on seniority provisions of union contracts. After five to fifteen years, those who start as copilot advance according to seniority to captain. Seniority also determines which pilots get the more desirable routes. In a nonairline job, a copilot may advance to pilot and, in large companies, to chief pilot or director of aviation in charge of aircraft, maintenance, and flight procedures. Merit can be more important than seniority for corporate pilots in climbing up the career ladder, while seniority is usually important for helicopter pilots.

SALARY AND BENEFITS

One of the best-paid positions in the travel, tourism, and hospitality industry is that of airline pilot. Captains' salaries at major airlines range from $73,000 to $300,000 annually. The salary range for captains at smaller airlines ranges from $20,000 to $151,000.

Earnings for copilots also vary depending on place of employment. Beginning salaries at major airlines range from $26,000 to $224,000. Beginning salaries at smaller airlines range from $12,000 to $73,000, depending on the size of the airplane flown. The number of flight engineers continues to dwindle dramatically, and entry-level wages for this position range from $23,000 to $61,000.

Typically, pilots working outside the airlines earn lower salaries. The average annual salary of commercial pilots is close to $50,000. The lowest 10 percent earn less than $30,000, while the highest 10 percent earn more than $100,000.

Airline pilots generally are eligible for life and health insurance plans paid for by the airlines as well as retirement benefits. If they should fail the FAA physical examination at some point in their careers, they get disability payments. In addition, pilots and their immediate families are usually entitled to free or reduced-fare transportation on their own and other airlines.

THE PERSONAL STORY OF A PILOT

An interest in flying in college has turned into a career as a pilot for Kit Darby. During his eight years in the military, he received an airline transport certificate, so he was qualified to seek a job with an airline upon returning to civilian life. His first job was with a flight training company, where he taught various aspects of flying and also obtained a rating to fly 727s. Within a few months, he landed a job with Braniff and began the company's training program: ground school for about four weeks, a flight simulator for almost two weeks, and twenty-five hours flying in the cockpit with experienced Braniff pilots.

Kit was briefly assigned to a B-727 as a flight engineer before he began flying DC-8s. After nine months, he became a copilot. Unfortunately, deregulation brought increasing financial difficulties to Braniff, and Kit was furloughed. He worked for a series of airlines over the next several years, ultimately taking a job at United as a flight engineer. After four years in this position on a B-727, he served as a copilot for three years, then became a B-737 captain.

Kit sees being a pilot as a blend of headwork and handwork. When flying is automated, he must constantly be monitoring what is happening. When he is hand-flying the plane, it is close to being a sport. Kit believes that, because of his love of flying, he is being paid to enjoy himself.

THE FUTURE

A mixed picture is emerging in the airline industry. A number of major airlines laid off pilots after the terrorist attacks on September 11, 2001. At the same time, hiring continued at regional and low-fare airlines. It is anticipated that job opportunities for pilots will continue to be better with these smaller airline companies than with the major airlines. Opportunities for employment with cargo air carriers should also be good. Overall, the employment of aircraft pilots should increase about as fast as most occupations through 2012. In the long run, the picture is bright as more people fly and the economy improves. In the short run, employment ties closely to swings in the economy between recession and prosperity.

Pilots applying for jobs at major airlines will face strong competition, as those companies attract more candidates when they have jobs. They also will be competing with laid-off pilots. Pilots who have logged the greatest number of flying hours on more sophisticated equipment will have the best chance of securing jobs. Prospects will also be good for job seekers with the most FAA licenses. Most likely, new two-pilot aircraft with computerized flight management systems will all but eliminate the demand for flight engineers.

FOR MORE INFORMATION

Before getting started on a career as a pilot, it is often helpful to visit the nearest airport to talk with a flight instructor. The Air Line Pilots Association also has a booklet for young people interested in aviation careers, available at alpa.org.

Aviation Information Resources, Inc., (AIR, Inc.) has an airline pilot starter kit with career information for a fee. The organization also has books as well as a monthly publication on airline careers. Write or visit the website to learn more about these materials:

Aviation Information Resources, Inc.
3800 Camp Creek Parkway, Suite 18-106
Atlanta, GA 30331
jet-jobs.com

The Federal Aviation Administration offers educational resources. It also sponsors weeklong summer aviation education programs for middle and high school students.

Director of Education
Department of Transportation
Federal Aviation Administration
800 Independence Avenue, SW
Washington, DC 20591
faa.gov

For information about employment with a specific airline, contact the airline's human resources department (see Appendix B).

LOOKING AT A CAREER AS A FLIGHT ATTENDANT

While the image of a flight attendant is that of a glamorous individual in uniform who travels to places most people dream of visiting, the reality is a hardworking individual who must ensure that all passengers have a safe, comfortable, and enjoyable flight. At various times, this job means being a nanny, a short-order cook, a waiter, a bartender, a psychologist, an instructor, a janitor, a librarian, a linguist, an emergency coordinator, a travel consultant, and even a paramedic. But the combination of free time and free or reduced airfares offered by this profession also provides great opportunities to travel and see new places.

WORKING CONDITIONS

Flight attendants may find themselves on small commuter planes with ten or fewer passengers or on jumbo jets with close to five hundred people on board. Attendants must be prepared to work at night, on holidays, and on weekends. They usually fly an average of sixty-five to eighty-five hours a month and spend about fifty hours on the ground preparing planes for flights, writing reports following completed flights, and waiting for planes that arrive late. During very long flights, they may have breaks to rest. Because of the way flights are scheduled and the limitations on their flying time, attendants can have considerable time off each month.

Flight attendants have a home base that is typically a major city, such as New York, San Francisco, or Atlanta. Attendants may be away from their home base at least one-third of the time. During layovers, the airlines provide transportation to and from airports, hotel accommodations, and an allowance for meal expenses. To be home every night, it is usually necessary to fly short routes for feeder airlines.

Being a flight attendant can be strenuous and trying work. Short flights require speedy service if meals are served. And full flights on small planes can make it difficult to maneuver food and drink carts in the aisles. A turbulent flight can also make serving food and drinks difficult. Flight attendants may suffer jet lag on long flights, and they are susceptible to injury because of the job demands in a moving aircraft. There is also the risk of exposure to contagious illnesses from being in close contact with so many people in a confined area.

RESPONSIBILITIES

A flight attendant arrives at the airport at least an hour before the plane is scheduled to depart. He or she attends a flight briefing with the other attendants at which responsibilities are assigned by the lead attendant, or purser.

Other issues, such as passengers with special needs or problems with the plane, are also discussed at this meeting.

Once aboard the plane, flight attendants typically have these responsibilities before takeoff: seeing that the passenger cabin is in order; checking that supplies of food, beverages, blankets, and reading materials are adequate; making sure that first-aid kits and other emergency equipment are aboard and in working order; greeting passengers and helping them find their seats; assisting passengers in storing coats and carry-on luggage; passing out newspapers and magazines; instructing passengers in the use of emergency equipment and the location of emergency exits; and checking that all seat belts are fastened, seat backs are forward, and tray tables are stored.

Once the plane is airborne, flight attendants try to make the passengers' trip enjoyable by answering questions about the flight and its arrival, connections, and the destination; distributing pillows, blankets, and headphones for movies; helping care for small children, the elderly, and disabled persons; serving cocktails and other refreshments; and preparing and distributing premade meals or snacks. On international flights, attendants also sell duty-free items and help passengers fill out entry and custom forms.

Before landing, attendants pick up headsets, gather trash, and check that the passengers have fastened their seat belts, stowed items away, and returned their seats and trays to their original positions. After landing, they help passengers deplane, prepare necessary reports, and straighten up the plane's cabin.

The most important responsibility of a flight attendant is to help passengers in the event of an emergency. This may range from reassuring passengers during occasional encounters with strong turbulence to directing passengers in evacuating a plane following an emergency landing.

PREPARATION FOR BECOMING A FLIGHT ATTENDANT

Most large airlines require that newly hired flight attendants complete three to eight weeks of intensive training in their own schools. Airlines that do not operate schools generally send new employees to the school of another airline. Trainees learn emergency procedures, such as evacuating an airplane, operating an oxygen system, and giving first aid. They are also taught flight regulations and duties and company operations and policy. Trainees learn how to prepare meals, handle the beverage service, speak on the intercom, and relate effectively with passengers. Instruction is also given on personal grooming. Toward the end of their training, students go on practice flights. Flight attendants who will be flying international routes get additional instruction in passport and customs regulations and dealing with terrorism. Throughout their careers, flight attendants are required to go through periodic retraining and to pass a FAA safety examination to continue flying.

SPECIAL ATTRIBUTES OF FLIGHT ATTENDANTS

Airlines want to hire poised, tactful, friendly, and resourceful men and women who deal comfortably with strangers. They also look for people who stay calm in emergencies and reassure others. Airlines prefer candidates who have several years of college or experience in dealing with the public. For international routes, a knowledge of a foreign language may be essential. Furthermore, applicants must fall into a specific weight range depending upon their height, have excellent health and good vision, and speak clearly.

ADVANCEMENT

After training, flight attendants are assigned to one of their airline's bases as reserve flight attendants, where they do not have regular assignments but are called on to staff extra flights or to fill in for attendants who are sick or on vacation. Reserve attendants on duty must be ready to fly on short notice. New attendants usually remain on reserve for at least one year; in some cities, however, it may take up to five years or longer to advance beyond reserve status. The length of time depends on the airline and on the routes that the reserve attendant flies. Once attendants are no longer on reserve, they bid for assignments on a seniority basis. Usually, only the most experienced attendants get their choice of base and flight.

The first step in advancement is to become a lead attendant in charge of the other attendants on the flight. Some airlines also have pursers, who are in charge of all the money collected during a flight. Beyond that, flight attendants must move into nonflight positions, such as instructor, supervisor, or recruiter, or into jobs involving contact with the public, such as reservation ticket agent or public relations specialist.

SALARY AND BENEFITS

While the average annual earnings of flight attendants is more than $40,000 a year, beginning flight attendants earn less than $20,000 per year. Pay scales, however, vary by carrier. Extra compensation is paid for overtime and for night and international flights. Benefits packages are also offered, including health insurance and pension plans. Most flight attendants belong to unions, which have helped secure improved salaries and benefits as well as recognition of the professionalism of this career. Flight attendants and their families are usually entitled to free or reduced fares on their own and most other airlines.

THE PERSONAL STORY OF A FLIGHT ATTENDANT

A chance meeting at a party with someone working in personnel at a major airline led to Christine Sydneysmith's career as a flight attendant. The airline needed attendants who were nurses, and Christine was just completing her R.N. degree. Within days, she went through the interview process and had secured a position. After completing company training, Christine was assigned to Los Angeles where she flew planes as a reserve flight attendant. She soon flew to Hawaii, as an R.N. was needed on those flights. Airlines are no longer required to have nurses on long overwater flights, but her training has given her the confidence to easily handle several medical emergencies. After Los Angeles, Christine was transferred to Detroit and then to New York, where she flew domestic routes. Today, Christine is based in Seattle and flies to Tokyo five times a month.

Besides being a flight attendant, Christine is very active in union activities. For years, she has been an alternate to the Board of Adjustment, which settles disputes between flight attendants and the company through arbitration. Christine was also the Employee Assistance Program representative for the flight attendants stationed in Seattle. This program offers confidential information and referrals to organizations that can help flight attendants with life's problems as well as emotional debriefing after aircraft emergencies.

The terrorist events of September 11 have affected Christine's work. Before the attack, she received instruction on how to handle hijackers and could enlist the help of the pilots. Now, she must be far more observant of passengers' behavior and is expected to be more assertive and aggressive in handling any incident, as attendants can no longer depend on any help from the cockpit. All flight attendants must be fingerprinted and have a clean FBI record.

THE FUTURE

Turnover was once very high among flight attendants. This is no longer the case because this occupation has become more professional. Nevertheless, the majority of job openings still come from the need to replace attendants who leave the labor force or transfer to other occupations. Overall, opportunities for individuals seeking positions as flight attendants have improved as more people return to the air after the terrorist attacks and the economic downturn. Employment of flight attendants is expected to grow about the same as the average of all occupations through the year 2012. Competition for jobs as flight attendants will remain very stiff because the number of applicants exceeds the number of job openings.

FOR MORE INFORMATION

To learn about job opportunities as a flight attendant at a particular airline and the qualifications required, check its website. Appendix B has a list of airlines and their addresses.

CHAPTER

4

CAREERS AS A RESERVATIONIST, CUSTOMER SERVICE REPRESENTATIVE, MECHANIC, AND IN OTHER AIRLINE JOBS

Most people in the airline industry work in what are called ground occupations. Reservationists typically talk to airline passengers over the phone, while ticket agents work at the airport. Airline mechanics maintain and repair aircraft to ensure the safety of their flights. Customer service representatives provide a variety of services at the airport, including selling tickets. Baggage handlers get luggage to passengers. Aircraft cleaners keep the interiors of planes in tip-top shape. There are also positions in management and in office and administrative support.

LOOKING AT A CAREER AS A RESERVATIONIST

Reservationists play an essential role in the transportation industry. They ensure that there will be seats on planes, trains, and buses; cabins on cruise ships; rooms at hotels and motels; and rental cars for the travelers who need them. The majority of reservationists are employed by airlines, but cruise lines, railroads, bus companies, tour companies, hotels and motels, travel agencies, and car rental companies also employ reservationists. And some reservationists work for membership organizations, such as automobile clubs, that provide transportation services.

WORKING CONDITIONS

Reservation agents usually work in large central offices. While these offices used to be in the downtown areas of major cities, increasingly they are found in suburban areas and even rural areas where rents are cheaper and travel companies can economize. On the job, most reservationists wear headsets all day so they can take calls from customers. Some may answer e-mail inquiries. They generally have computer terminals so they can quickly obtain information to make, change, or cancel reservations at the customer's request. Their workplace is loud, as it is filled with the voices of other reservationists and the clicking of computer keys. There isn't much privacy in these offices, although some reservationists have their own cubicles.

Most reservationists work eight or eight and a half hours a day, five days a week. Because airlines and other travel companies keep their phone lines open twenty-four hours a day, reservationists often work shifts. Beginning workers typically have the least desirable shifts, because reservationists bid for their work times based on seniority. Some overtime work should be expected, especially around holidays and when travel promotions are offered. Many airline reservationists are part-time employees who may work full-time during sales promotions or periods of high demand.

RESPONSIBILITIES

Each phone call connects reservationists to new customers who request their help. Typically, reservationists answer customers' questions, offer suggestions on travel arrangements, and provide information about fares, schedules, and the booking of flights, trips, cruises, accommodations, or rental cars. They then book reservations and arrange for tickets to be mailed, picked up, or handled as ticketless travel. In the process, they compile and record reservation information, confirm or change travel reservations, and record methods of payment. To fulfill these duties, reservationists must keep up with the latest changes in fares, schedules, and other arrangements.

PREPARATION FOR BECOMING A RESERVATIONIST

No matter where a reservationist elects to work, he or she will have on-the-job training to learn the company's product, automated reservations system, and sales procedures. Travel school or community college courses in using a reservations system may be required to obtain jobs with many companies. Reservationists must be good typists. In addition, companies like to hire individuals who have sales experience. Knowing how to use a computer is definitely helpful, and a college degree is also an advantage in this job market.

SPECIAL ATTRIBUTES OF RESERVATIONISTS

Not everyone has the aptitude to be a reservationist. For this job, it is absolutely essential to work fast and accurately and to deal effectively with people. During the course of the day, reservationists encounter difficult, indecisive, and belligerent customers whom they must convince to purchase their company's travel product. Being a reservationist is a job for a salesperson who can remain upbeat and enthusiastic through as many as several hundred customer calls in a day. This requires having a pleasant telephone manner and a thorough knowledge of the travel product.

ADVANCEMENT

No matter where reservationists work, they essentially do the same job. Some reservationists will move to other companies that offer more interesting assignments or better pay. Reservationists in large companies have the opportunity to transfer laterally into positions in international or frequent flyer travel or to advance to positions as senior agents, supervisors, or managers. Agents can also elect to move into another department in their company, such as sales and marketing, to advance their careers.

SALARY AND BENEFITS

Airlines once paid high salaries for reservationists; because of cost-cutting measures, however, this is no longer true at some airlines. Today, the average annual earnings in this occupation are close to $30,000. Experienced reservationists can make more than $40,000 a year, while the few who work overtime constantly (eighty-hour weeks) can earn up to $100,000. Full-time reservationists receive benefits such as health insurance, paid vacations, and discounted and free travel; part-time employees typically get only travel benefits.

THE PERSONAL STORY OF A RESERVATIONIST

Carol Love is an experienced reservationist who has worked in domestic, international, prepaid tickets, and group sales for a major airline. Her career began just before computers were incorporated into the job, and it wasn't until the mid-1980s that she began working on a totally modern system. Now she works on the most up-to-date computer reservations equipment in the airline industry. Over the years, Carol's job has become more complex because travelers' options have increased with the introduction of so many different fares and the greater number of flights to each destination.

Carol works in domestic sales. Her customers can be from anywhere in the United States, because the company routes calls between its six centers to balance the workload. The most common call she receives is from customers wanting to buy tickets. She also provides information to people who cannot or do not want to use the automated flight information system. During periods of bad weather, she answers a lot of questions about plane arrivals and departures and the cancellation of flights. And she refers callers who want to complain about or compliment airline employees or policies to customer relations.

Once Carol puts on her headphones and sits down in front of her computer terminal, the company expects her to be plugged into the phone 95 percent of the time when she is not on a break. The company keeps track of this, as well as how many seconds each call lasts. While the company goal is for agents to spend 180 seconds (three minutes) on a call, Carol usually averages 300 seconds (five minutes) per call. She spends this extra time because she wants to be sure her customers understand all aspects of purchasing a ticket, including whether the ticket can be changed or is refundable. Although Carol's call time is above average, this is not frowned upon by the company because she sells a lot of tickets. Once her shift begins, the phone calls never stop coming. This is a job that truly requires employees to stay on task.

Carol enjoys her job as a reservationist. The money is great, and she loves the flexibility of shift work, which has allowed her to get a college degree as well as take classes in personal interests like photography. Having a six-week paid vacation is another benefit of this job, along with the ability to change shifts and days and to travel worldwide at a nominal cost.

LOOKING AT A CAREER AS A CUSTOMER SERVICE REPRESENTATIVE

Customer service representatives are the smartly uniformed individuals who deal directly with the public. At airlines, they are the employees behind the ticket counter, at the gate, in baggage service, at the ramp, and in the baggage room. They are also the people behind the counter at car rental sites and central city ticket offices. Depending on their job responsibilities, they are known as customer service agents, ticket agents, passenger agents, gate agents, passenger-booking clerks, ticket sellers, ramp agents, or baggage agents. No matter what their title is, they help smooth the way for travelers.

RESPONSIBILITIES

Customer service representatives at major air terminals are not likely to have as wide a range of duties each day as those at small terminals. Depending on the airline, customer service representatives may alternate where they work or be permanently assigned to one station. Customer service representatives may be called upon to handle many tasks. They provide information about fares, schedules, and flights and sell tickets. They check in passengers, examine passports and/or visas, and issue boarding passes. They may also make boarding announcements, collect tickets at the gate, and help passengers board. They may check, load, and unload luggage. They also assist passengers who are elderly or disabled, children, and passengers who become ill or injured. They direct the arrival and departure of planes. And they resolve problems ranging from lost luggage to medical emergencies.

PREPARATION FOR BECOMING A CUSTOMER SERVICE REPRESENTATIVE

Typically, customer service representatives learn their job through formal training programs and on-the-job training after they are hired. Computer skills are a necessity for many of the tasks customer service representatives handle, and a certain amount of physical strength may be required because lifting luggage is often part of this job.

SALARY, BENEFITS, AND ADVANCEMENT

Customer service representatives generally start as probationary employees and become part-time employees before achieving full-time status. The average annual earnings for customer service representatives working in air transportation, at $28,000, is higher than in other workplaces. Full-time employees typically receive health, vacation, and travel benefits. Part-time employees usually receive travel benefits but may not be eligible for other benefits.

Job assignments are based on seniority, and employees bid for the shifts that they want. They can generally switch with other customer service representatives to get the work hours and work assignments they want. Like reservationists, they can become supervisors and then managers if they wish to advance.

THE PERSONAL STORY OF A CUSTOMER SERVICE REPRESENTATIVE

Cynthia Jones (not her real name) is thoroughly delighted with her job of more than five years as a customer service representative. It lets her travel (she especially enjoys trips to Hawaii and Europe), use her knowledge of Spanish, and deal with the public. Before finding what she calls her perfect career niche, this college graduate worked at a bank, a wind energy company, and a pharmaceuticals firm. She sees herself working in her current job for many years.

Cynthia started her customer service career as a ramper (also known as ramp agent). This began after forty hours of training, followed by on-the-job training. Rampers have various tasks, from paperwork and the arrangement of the cargo to marshalling the plane in with wands, connecting ground power, and loading and unloading baggage. To be a ramper requires a certain amount of physical strength; Cynthia had to demonstrate that she could pick up seventy pounds and turn around while holding it. After a ninety-day probationary period, Cynthia worked part-time for a month before becoming a full-time employee.

Cynthia's employer likes its customer service representatives to be cross-utilized—that is, capable of handling several of the jobs that these representatives customarily do. Thus, Cynthia works a variety of services. On baggage service, she finds it challenging to find missing baggage and assuage unhappy travelers. At the ticket counter, she has no idea whether she will be issuing or reissuing tickets, making a reservation, checking in a passenger, or handling a more complicated request for each customer. In the baggage room, Cynthia takes baggage off the belt and places it in the appropriate cart by flight and destination. Then she drives each cart to a plane, where she may help load the luggage. When she is working at the gate, she checks in passengers; makes announcements; assists the elderly, children, and disabled to board; tears the ticket stubs of boarding passengers; and reconciles the tickets to the number of passengers on the plane.

Throughout her career as a customer service representative, Cynthia has continually received training, because changes are constantly being made in procedures ranging from security to baggage handling. She has also taken part in motivation programs offered at the company headquarters. Furthermore, Cynthia can expect occasional Federal Aviation Administration (FAA) checks that make sure her company is complying with all airline regulations.

THE FUTURE FOR RESERVATIONISTS AND CUSTOMER SERVICE REPRESENTATIVES

Most applicants for positions as reservationists and customer service representatives are likely to encounter considerable competition for jobs because the supply of qualified applicants exceeds the demand. Many people satisfy the entry requirements, and many applicants are attracted to these jobs by the travel benefits and the glamour associated with the industry. The number of reservation and ticket agents will grow more slowly than the average as airlines phase out paper tickets and move to electronic tickets over the Internet. However, the safety and security responsibilities of these two jobs will prevent a decline in these jobs.

FOR MORE INFORMATION

For information about job opportunities as a reservationist or as a customer service representative, write to the human resources departments of individual airlines (see Appendix B).

37

Careers as a
Reservationist, Customer
Service Representative,
Mechanic, and in Other
Airline Jobs

LOOKING AT A CAREER AS AN AIRLINE MECHANIC

About 40 percent of all aircraft mechanics work for air transportation companies and close to 20 percent work for private maintenance and repair facilities; the rest work for the federal government, aerospace companies, and companies that operate their own planes. Most aircraft mechanics work at major airports near large cities. Their workdays will usually be spent in hangars or in other indoor areas unless they have to make immediate repairs or preflight checks on aircraft, which can put them outside in very unpleasant weather. Airline mechanics frequently work under time pressure to maintain flight schedules. At the same time, they have the overwhelming responsibility to maintain safety standards.

Mechanics generally work forty hours a week on eight-hour shifts around the clock, and overtime work is frequent. Their work often involves standing, lying, or kneeling in awkward positions to do inspections, maintenance, and repair work; occasionally, they work in precarious positions on scaffolds or ladders.

RESPONSIBILITIES

Mechanics have the responsibility of keeping aircraft in peak operating condition by performing scheduled maintenance, making repairs, and completing inspections required by the FAA. Maintenance work involves inspecting such things as engines, landing gear, instruments, pressurized sections, brakes, valves, pumps, and air-conditioning systems and then doing the necessary maintenance. Mechanics may need to remove an engine from a plane and take it apart, then use precision instruments to check it for wear or x-ray and magnetic inspection equipment to check for invisible cracks. Maintenance workers also check the fuselage, wings, and tail for corrosion, distortion, and cracks. Once all of the repairs are completed, the mechanics have to test that everything is working properly. While mechanics who do maintenance work are following a set protocol, those who do repair work rely on pilots' descriptions of problems to find and fix faulty equipment. These mechanics must work as fast as safety permits so that the aircraft can quickly be put back into service.

Mechanics may work on one or many types of aircraft or specialize in one area of a particular aircraft, such as the engine, electrical system, or air-conditioning system. Because of technological advances, mechanics now spend more time repairing electronic systems.

Besides mechanics, many other airline employees work on the maintenance and repair of aircraft. Included in this group are machinists, sheet metal workers, carpenters, electricians, painters, electroplaters, drill press operators, and upholsterers.

PREPARATION FOR BECOMING A MECHANIC

Some individuals still become aircraft mechanics through on-the-job training, but most learn their jobs in FAA-certified trade schools. Emphasis in these schools is placed on technologies such as turbine engines, aviation electronics, and composite materials, including graphite, fiberglass, and boron, which are being used more and more in the construction of new aircraft. Completing a course generally takes from twenty-four to thirty months.

Certain high school and college courses—including mathematics, physics, chemistry, electronics, computer science, and mechanical drawing—are quite helpful to future mechanics, because knowledge of their principles is often necessary to make repairs. Writing skills are also important because mechanics are frequently required to submit reports. Furthermore, as aircraft continue to become more complex, airlines are requiring mechanics to take ongoing training to update their skills, especially in electronics.

The majority of airline mechanics are certified by the FAA as airframe mechanic, powerplant mechanic, or avionics repair specialists. Airframe mechanics are authorized to work on any part of the aircraft except the instruments, powerplants, and propellers. Powerplant mechanics are authorized to work on engines and to do limited work on propellers. Avionics repairers have the authorization to work on instruments and on propellers. Most airline mechanics are combination airframe and powerplant mechanics, or A & P mechanics, and can work on all parts of a plane except instruments. Those with an inspector's authorization can certify inspection work completed by other mechanics as well as perform required inspections. Uncertified mechanics are supervised by certified mechanics.

SPECIAL ATTRIBUTES OF AN AIRLINE MECHANIC

Individuals must do careful and thorough work as the safety of so many individuals depends on their work. Airline mechanics must have a high degree of mechanical aptitude because they have to diagnose and solve complex mechanical problems. They also need to be self-motivated, hardworking, and enthusiastic. Moreover, they need to be agile to handle all of the reaching and climbing that are part of this job. And because they work high off the ground, on top of the wings and fuselages of large jets, these mechanics must not be afraid of heights.

ADVANCEMENT

In the airlines, the promotion of mechanics is often determined by examination and experience. Opportunities are best for those who have an aircraft inspector's authorization. Mechanics can climb the career ladder to become lead mechanics (crew chiefs), inspectors, lead inspectors, and shop supervisors. Supervisors may advance to executive positions. Those with broad experience in maintenance and overhaul might become inspectors with the FAA.

SALARY AND BENEFITS

Mechanics who work on jets for the major airlines generally earn more than those who work on other aircraft. The median annual earnings for aircraft mechanics and service technicians, at more than $48,000 per year, is second only to pilots in this industry. Mechanics are paid an hourly rate that can top $29 per hour. They also work considerable overtime. Some mechanics at major airlines are covered by union agreements. Airline mechanics also have travel benefits along with health insurance and vacation benefits.

THE FUTURE FOR AIRLINE MECHANICS

41

Careers as a
Reservationist, Customer
Service Representative,
Mechanic, and in Other
Airline Jobs

Employment opportunities for aircraft equipment mechanics and technicians are excellent. Furthermore, fewer entrants from the military and a large number of retirements indicate excellent opportunities for students just beginning technician training.

FOR MORE INFORMATION

For general information and scholarships, contact:

Professional Aviation Maintenance Association
717 Princess Street
Alexandria, VA 22314
pama.org

For information about jobs at a particular airline, write to the company's personnel manager (see Appendix B).

LOOKING AT OTHER AIRLINE JOBS

Within the very large airline industry, many jobs allow employees to travel besides pilot or flight attendant. In fact, every airline offers flight benefits to its full-time employees and most part-time employees, which means that airline secretaries, accountants, computer operators, and lawyers can take frequent trips. Furthermore, within every airline, individuals can find jobs in technology, research, marketing, sales, human resources, public relations, law, operations, advertising, administration, and finance that offer the additional benefit of travel. In each area, there are entry-level, middle-management, and senior-management positions.

CAREERS ABOARD CRUISE SHIPS

Salt spray in the wind, the rocking motion of a ship, and maritime traditions have always lured sailors to sea. You can experience that life as an employee on a cruise ship because millions of people are cruising each year. In fact, the building of cruise ships has so accelerated in recent years that sixty-two new ships were built between 2000 and 2004, and more will be launched in the future. Cruising offers the possibility of visiting exotic locales; eating gourmet meals; enjoying endless shipboard entertainment, including shows, movies, dancing, lectures, games, gambling, health spas, and sports; and participating in special interest activities like photography and scrapbooking. Themed cruises are also available for those who want to focus on cooking, gardening, or a specific culture.

Cruises can last for just a day, a more popular three to five days, one or two weeks, or even several months. And cruise ships are rapidly expanding their ports of call to more and more cities in the United States, such as New York City, Charleston, and Baltimore, as well as to new ports around the world. Today's cruise ships vary greatly in size, from large oceangoing ships that carry several thousand passengers to small ships with less than one hundred passengers cruising inland bodies of water and less-visited locales. Cruising opportunities are also available on much smaller barges and on sailboats.

LOOKING AT JOBS ABOARD CRUISE SHIPS

Very few cruise ships are United States ships, as it is more expensive to build ships in the United States and to staff them with North Americans than to build them elsewhere and hire non-Americans. Most crew members aboard a ship—one for every two or three passengers—are not American. Typically, the officers are from European countries, such as England, Italy, Greece, and Norway, and the staff in such employee-intensive departments as food and beverage, hotel, deck, and engine are from Asia. Because the majority of passengers are from North America, most job opportunities for Americans are in positions that deal directly with passengers, such as cruise staff, the purser's staff, and service jobs such as gift-shop personnel, beauticians, casino dealers, naturalists, tour guides, and photographers as well as those helping passengers indulge in their special interests. Only cruise ships that fly the American flag, including all ships cruising the inland waters of the United States, will have exclusively American crews.

WORKING CONDITIONS

The ship is the home of those who work aboard it. Employees, depending upon their positions, may have to share cabins that are far more spartan than those the passengers enjoy. Newer ships have amenities like employee cabins with their own bathrooms and even television sets; they may also have employee stores, pantries, laundries, and recreation lounges. Employee quarters are usually on one of the crew decks; however, some cruise staff on the larger ships may be in the more luxurious passenger areas. Most cruise-ship employees eat in crew messes, which may offer different cuisines ranging from Asian to American. However, the ship's officers and some members of the cruise staff regularly eat with passengers. They are the only employees that generally have access to passenger areas when not working.

Aboard the ship, most employees wear uniforms associated with their jobs. While cruises are a true vacation for passengers, they may require long hours, seven days a week, for employees. It is not unusual for employees to have to work ten to fifteen hours a day with no time off for three to nine months, depending on their contracts. How much an employee works depends solely on his or her job. Waiters work long hours, while manicurists, musicians, and photographers may work relatively short hours. The marine crew, which includes the deck and engine departments, work regularly scheduled hours.

There are no long layovers for rests in ports. Typically, ships leave a home port and then stop in different ports before returning to one of several home ports. Passengers disembark in the morning on the last day of a cruise, and new passengers come aboard that same afternoon. Then the ship takes off on the same itinerary or a new one.

RESPONSIBILITIES BY DEPARTMENT

Jobs are much the same from one cruise ship to the next. However, cruise lines will assign responsibilities to different departments and staff members. What follows is a general description of the departments found on cruise ships and the positions in these departments, along with the employees' duties.

Deck

The deck department personnel operate and navigate the ship and handle all sea duties, as well as maintain the ship. Passengers see deck personnel when they visit the bridge, when the ship is tied to docks, when lifeboat drills are held, and when some of the officers eat with the passengers. The captain is the head of this department, and all other department heads report to the captain. Positions in this department include ordinary seaman and able seaman as well as marine officers.

Engine

The engine department staff operates, maintains, and repairs the engines that propel the ship. They are also responsible for all the electrical, plumbing, and mechanical systems on the ship. The chief engineer is in charge of this department. Within this department, there are first, second, third, and fourth engineers; electricians; plumbers; machinists; welders; and mechanics.

Food and Beverage

Employees of the food and beverage department have much the same titles and duties as they would in a first-class hotel. This is the largest department on a cruise ship and an extremely important one, because passengers will not make repeat trips with a cruise line unless the food is outstanding and the servers helpful and friendly. The chief steward, or food and beverage manager, is in charge of the entire operation and is responsible for making menus, purchasing food and beverages, and handling all dining room and bar services. On the food side, some of the positions are:

assistant chefs	dining room manager
assistant maitre d'	dishwashers
bussers	food handlers
butchers	maitre d'
chefs	specialized cooks
cooks	waitstaff

On every cruise ship, the bar is one of the profit makers. Again, the friendliness and competence of this staff is extremely important. The beverage staff includes these positions:

assistant bar manager	dishwashers
bar manager	waitstaff
bartenders	wine stewards
chief wine steward	

Hotel

The hotel department workers comprise the second largest department on cruise ships. Heading the department is a hotel manager who is responsible for every passenger's comfort, the employees in this area, and the cleanliness of the ship as well as obtaining the necessary supplies and amenities for every cabin. Working in this department are the chief steward (housekeeper), room stewards, cleaners, and bellhops.

Purser

Employees in the purser's department are ship's officers who wear uniforms at all times. The chief purser and his or her assistants handle all of the administrative tasks related to the passengers. They provide such services as cashing checks, staffing the ship's information desk, running the lost-and-found department, storing valuables, handling complaints, changing cabins for passengers, doing the ship's accounting, maintaining accurate passenger records, providing translators, dealing with customs officials, and handling embarkation and disembarkation.

Cruise

The cruise department has the task of entertaining the passengers. These employees lead and implement all daily recreational activities, including shipboard activities, shore excursions, and entertainment. The cruise director heads this department and has a staff of assistants, including hosts and hostesses, a shore excursion director, a recreation director, a children's activities coordinator, musicians and entertainers, and staff to set up the various activities. Members of this staff wear uniforms and have access to all the public areas aboard the ship when in uniform. They may be assigned to eat with the passengers. They must be gregarious people who are at home speaking with one person or five hundred people.

Service

The service department staff on cruise ships includes all those who offer services as photographers, gift-shop employees, beauticians, barbers, manicurists, masseuses and masseurs, doctors and other health personnel, and casino dealers and cashiers. These individuals may be hired by the cruise lines but may also be hired by companies that operate these concessions aboard the ship. Their duties are the same as they would be on shore.

PREPARATION FOR BECOMING A CRUISE-SHIP EMPLOYEE

Cruise lines look for experienced employees. They want chefs who have worked in first-class restaurants, stewards in housekeeping with work experience in hotels, and musicians who have been in organized groups. Certain employees, including doctors, nurses, and barbers and beauticians, need to have experience plus the appropriate licenses to obtain jobs.

Deck and engineering officers aboard United States cruise ships must be licensed. To qualify for a license, applicants must have graduated from the U.S. Merchant Marine Academy or one of the six state academies and passed a written examination. Individuals without formal training can be licensed if they pass the written examination and possess sea service appropriate to the license for which they are applying. It is quite difficult to pass the examination without substantial formal schooling or independent study, and it may take years to get the necessary experience. The academies offer four-year programs leading to a bachelor degree and a license (issued only by the Coast Guard) as a third mate (deck officer) or third assistant engineer (engineering officer). By gaining experience and passing additional examinations, third officers may qualify for higher rank. Deck and engineering officers who seek employment with foreign-flagged ships must demonstrate naval skill and show proof of attendance at an accredited school or a license acceptable to the cruise company. Even sailors and unlicensed engineers on U.S. ships must hold a Coast Guard–issued document.

ADVANCEMENT

To advance up the career ladder, it is essential to work for a cruise line for longer than a few months. Even those who are experienced in the hotel or restaurant field on land may find it necessary to take a lower starting position than the one they held on shore. Because there is considerable turnover, however, individuals can begin in entry-level positions in most departments and advance rather rapidly into management jobs. Incidentally, most employees who advance to on-shore positions with cruise companies have spent some time working aboard ships.

SALARY AND BENEFITS

To many Americans, the pay aboard cruise ships for many positions is considered low. However, to those from third world and some European countries, who make up the majority of the employees, these wages are better than what they could earn at home. The amount of money that cruise staff members earn depends on their position and the cruise line that they work for. There is a wide range between entry-level and top salaries. For example, in housekeeping, a chief housekeeper could earn close to $4,000 per month based on salary and a share of tips, while a cleaner could earn as little as $600 per month including tips. Bar staff members also depend on tips and earn between $1,000 and $3,000 per month. Those who work in the retail shops depend on commissions from the shops' profits. Waitstaff and bussers generally receive very low wages, sometimes less than $100 a month, but may make very good income from tips. Americans are most likely to work in the cruise department for higher wages. American cruise lines that have unionized employees pay higher salaries.

Many fringe benefits allow cruise employees to save a considerable portion of their wages. First, there is free room and board and laundry service for the duration of employment. Uniforms are usually furnished by the cruise line, while employees who are asked to wear a certain type of garb may have a clothes allowance. Employees receive free medical service aboard the ship. Vacation time is also provided by many lines after a certain period of service.

PERKS AND PRESSURES OF BEING A CRUISE-SHIP EMPLOYEE

This job has one outstanding perk—free travel. Cruise-ship employees can truly see the world. After being employed for a certain length of time, employees can have guests aboard (family and, in some cases, friends) for a very nominal daily fee. Some companies also have interline agreements that let employees travel on other cruise ships for a very low daily charge. Other perks are the opportunity to work with people from many different countries and to meet travelers with diverse interests and occupations. Plus, as staff typically work on contracts of three to nine months, it is possible to have vacations of several weeks or more.

There are downsides to working aboard cruise ships, too. Employees must always exhibit a sunny personality to passengers. Besides the low pay and long hours, most employees are limited to crew areas in their off hours. In addition, very few employees are able to participate in on-board ship activities or to go ashore in every port. And the military-like hierarchy of authority will not appeal to everyone.

THE PERSONAL STORY OF A CRUISE-SHIP EMPLOYEE

Julee Moser's first job was serving as a ship's secretary. Her major responsibility each day was to coordinate all of the events and write as well as print the daily program of activities for the ship. In the evening, she would host and mingle at cocktail parties and attend special events. Other duties included collecting passports, cruise documents, and tickets on embarkation days and helping direct passengers and luggage on disembarkation days.

Julee's second job was as an assistant shore excursion manager. Julee worked part of the time at a desk where she sold tickets for ports of call, answered questions about tours, and told people about local places and transportation. She also went on shore excursions, acting as a supervisor to ensure that everything was going as planned.

Julee then worked as a passenger service representative for four years. In this position, she would meet the passengers scheduled on her flight to the ship, fly with the passengers, clear customs, and help them board the ship. Aboard the ship, Julee's major responsibility was to prepare all the paperwork for the disembarkation of the passengers. At the end of the cruise, Julee held disembarkation briefings organized by airplane flights in which she would explain how to disembark the ship properly, give out all tickets and luggage tags, and make any corrections that were necessary.

Finally, Julee elected to become a future cruise consultant. While seated at a desk outside of the ship's dining room for two hours in the morning and two hours in the afternoon, she gave information to passengers about the cruise line's ships, prices and promotions, and space availability.

THE FUTURE

Because the number of cruise passengers keeps growing each year, as does the number of cruise ships, employment needs are steadily increasing. In fact, the opportunities for employment are great as each new ship generates between three hundred and one thousand more jobs. Furthermore, according to the president of Disney Cruise Lines, over 90 percent of those who can afford to take a cruise vacation have not done so, which means there is a very large population of potential cruisers. And once people take cruises, they are inclined to take another cruise within five years. Another factor affecting employment opportunities is the high turnover of employees. North Americans need to remember, however, that even though the number of employees on cruise ships is steadily increasing, the majority of employees aboard these ships are from other countries.

FOR MORE INFORMATION

Information on employment opportunities aboard cruise ships can be obtained by writing to the individual cruise lines or visiting their websites. The Cruise Lines International Association (CLIA) has a list of cruise lines and ship profiles at cruising.org. These lines are primarily located in New York, Miami, and Los Angeles. Good guides to getting a job with a cruise line are *How to Get a Job on a Cruise Ship* by Don Kennedy (Careersource Publications) and *How to Get a Job with a Cruise Line* by Mary Fallon Miller (Ticket to Adventure).

LOOKING AT OTHER OPPORTUNITIES IN THE CRUISE INDUSTRY

Most cruise industry jobs for North Americans are not aboard ships but in administration, sales, marketing, finance, management information systems, and operations within cruise companies. Most cruise lines offer their land-based employees cruises for a very nominal daily charge—or even free. In addition, some employees go aboard ships as part of their jobs. For example, employees in management information systems departments may need to install new or updated programs or systems on the ships' computers as well as update computer hardware.

CHAPTER 6

CAREERS WORKING IN EVEN MORE TRAVEL JOBS

Besides careers involving air and water travel, many travel careers are linked to land transportation, such as railroad travel and bus travel. In addition, many professions such as travel writer and travel photographer necessitate frequent travel to exotic locales. And jobs that involve opportunities for travel are certainly not limited to ones working with tourists or travelers. Some jobs with trucking firms involve almost constant travel. Many companies in the United States sell their products throughout the country and the world, necessitating considerable domestic and foreign travel for some employees. Hotels, fast-food chains, automobile manufacturers, and banks have offices throughout the world that need staffing. Furthermore, the United States government has employees in foreign embassies, and every branch of the armed services presents opportunities to live abroad.

LOOKING AT CAREERS WITH RAILROADS: AMTRAK

The railroads were once travelers' first choice for transportation in the United States. However, after World War II, most passengers deserted the railroads for buses and planes. In 1970, the federal government created Amtrak to preserve some passenger lines. The new corporation faced many obstacles, with poor roadbeds, old equipment, inadequate maintenance facilities, a weak ticketing system, and too many routes. Much progress in developing a modern passenger rail system has been made with the introduction of a computerized ticketing system, new cars, high-speed trains, improved roadbeds and facilities, and a reduced number of routes. The system currently operates 266 trains a day over a 23,800-mile system and serves 530 stations in 46 states. Since its inception, Amtrak has operated at a deficit and has been under continual pressure from the government to achieve profitability.

Individuals who have dreamed of a life riding the rails should look for jobs that involve traveling with Amtrak rather than with freight lines. Because of work rules, locomotive engineers and conductors on freight trains only work eight hours or 130 miles—whichever comes first. A freight trip may be as short as two or three hours and will not involve much true travel, as these employees remain within a district.

Engineers

In the cab of every Amtrak train, there are always two employees: the engineer and the assistant engineer. The engineer operates the train by using the throttle to start and accelerate the train and the brakes to slow and stop it. The assistant engineer watches the track and the signals that indicate track obstructions, other train movements, and speed limits and keeps in constant contact with the dispatcher and conductor by sending and receiving messages.

Engineer jobs are frequently filled by workers who have experience in other railroad-operating occupations. Beginning assistant engineers receive six weeks of instruction, which includes hands-on instruction in locomotive operation as well as instruction in operating rules and regulations. Seniority dictates advancement from newly trained engineer to assistant engineer to engineer.

Conductors

The responsibility for the safety and well-being of all passengers rests on the conductor. This individual has the following duties: handling tickets, supervising the boarding and detraining of passengers and any baggage, staying in radio contact with the cab, deciding in consultation with the engineer if a train with mechanical or other problems can continue its route, throwing switches, and deciding when a train can leave the station.

The conductor is usually aided by an assistant conductor. Conductors and assistant conductors are given extensive training that covers operations, emergency procedures, ticketing, and handling people.

Service Personnel

Aboard every long-distance train are such personnel as porters and dining car, lounge car, and sleeping car attendants. An onboard service chief is in charge of this entire crew. Occasionally, trains have guides calling attention to points of interest. These railroad jobs truly involve travel, because onboard service personnel work an entire trip cross-country or within a region.

SALARY AND BENEFITS

Almost all railroad transportation workers working aboard trains are members of unions. Amtrak assistant engineers earn approximately $34,000 per year, while engineers' salaries average close to $58,000. Assistant conductors earn an average salary of about $42,000 and conductors earn close to $49,000. Employees receive benefits including health insurance, vacation time, and personal days, and uniforms are provided. Reduced-price travel is available for all Amtrak employees and their spouses, and there are occasional free travel days.

THE FUTURE

The downsizing of Amtrak in the early 1990s, along with uncertainties about the ability of the corporation to reduce costs and receive government funding, make it difficult to predict what the demand for employees will be in the future. Most openings will arise as workers retire or leave jobs for other reasons.

LOOKING AT A CAREER AS A BUS DRIVER

The heyday for bus travel was the 1940s and 1950s. At that time, air service was limited and few families owned cars. As air travel became cheaper and more available and most families purchased cars, fewer and fewer people elected to use bus transportation between cities. Still, buses transport millions of Americans every day. Modern buses used on intercity routes and as tour buses and charters provide a very comfortable trip with their wide windows, reclining seats, air-conditioning, restrooms, viewing decks, and even movies. Furthermore, buses serve far more communities than the airlines and railroads do, at very low fares.

Bus deregulation in the 1980s brought about the creation of several thousand new companies. Greyhound is the only company that offers nationwide service. Most bus companies are primarily devoted to providing buses for tours and charters. And, of course, all major cities have scheduled routed bus routes within the city.

WORKING CONDITIONS

Because intercity, tour, and charter bus drivers truly spend their working days traveling, the focus of this section will be on them rather than on local route or school bus drivers. Charter and tour drivers, especially, have the opportunity to travel to popular tourist spots. Bus drivers may work nights, weekends, and holidays. They often spend nights away from home, staying at hotels at company expense. Intercity drivers with seniority have regular schedules, but others must be prepared to report to work on short notice. In addition, seasonal layoffs are common for some companies, such as during the winter when regular schedule, tour, and charter business falls off.

RESPONSIBILITIES

All bus drivers face driving through heavy traffic while dealing with passengers, which can be stressful. At the same time, they have the advantage of working long stretches without direct supervision. The length of the workday of bus drivers is strictly regulated by the Department of Transportation. All drivers must keep accurate logs of their duty time and driving time. Bus drivers must be alert to prevent accidents, especially in heavy traffic or in bad weather, and to avoid sudden stops or swerves that jar passengers.

Besides picking up and discharging passengers at terminals, intercity drivers collect fares; answer questions about schedules, routes, and transfer points; sometimes handle luggage; and sometimes announce stops. They must adhere to schedules. In a day, intercity drivers may make a single one-way trip to a distant city or a round trip to a nearer city. They may stop at towns just a few miles apart or at large cities hundreds of miles apart. Drivers who operate chartered buses pick up groups, take them to their destinations, and generally remain with them until they return, which could be the same day or a week or more later. Tour drivers drive an entire tour and can be gone as long as thirty days.

PREPARATION FOR BECOMING A BUS DRIVER

The first prerequisite for becoming a bus driver is to like to drive and travel. Once hired, drivers must secure a commercial driver's license from the state in which they live by taking a written test and passing a road test in the type of vehicle they will be operating. Drivers who will travel between states must meet Department of Transportation regulations. Many intercity bus companies prefer drivers who are high school graduates and at least twenty-four years of age, and some require several years of bus or truck driving experience. Prospective intercity drivers also are required to submit to drug screening. Companies also do a background check to make sure prospective drivers do not have a criminal record or serious driving violations. Intercity, tour, and charter companies expect their drivers to have well-developed people skills.

SALARY, BENEFITS, AND ADVANCEMENT

Beginning intercity drivers who work about six months out of the year will earn more than $20,000, while senior drivers who work all year can earn more than $48,000. With tips, charter and tour drivers can earn between $50,000 and $75,000 a year. Most intercity drivers receive paid health and life insurance, sick leave, and free bus rides on any of the regular routes of their line or system. Full-time drivers also get as much as four weeks of paid vacation annually.

Opportunities for promotion are generally limited. Experienced drivers may become supervisors or dispatchers, who assign buses to drivers, check whether drivers are on schedule, reroute buses to avoid traffic jams and other problems, and dispatch extra vehicles and service crew to scenes of accidents and breakdowns. A few drivers become instructors and managers.

THE FUTURE

Well-qualified applicants seeking jobs as bus drivers should find good opportunities. Employment of intercity drivers will grow as bus ridership increases because the population and labor force are growing and funding levels for public transport may be increasing. Nevertheless, there may continue to be competition for intercity bus drivers in some areas, since many of these positions offer relatively high wages and attractive benefits. The most competitive positions will offer regular hours and steady driving routes. There will also be an increase in group charters to locations not served by other modes of transportation as well as to tourist attractions.

LOOKING AT A CAREER AS A TRUCK DRIVER

There are more than two million truck drivers in the United States. Most of them have jobs concentrated in and around large cities. Only the long-distance truckers travel to distant areas of the country. On long runs, drivers may haul loads from city to city for a week or more before returning home. Some companies use two drivers on very long runs, allowing one driver to sleep in a berth while the other drives. Stops are made only for fuel, food, loading, and unloading.

RESPONSIBILITIES

Long-distance truck drivers spend most of their time behind the wheel but may be required to unload their cargo. Before beginning their trip, they check their trucks for fuel and oil; make sure the brakes, windshield wipers, and lights are working, and verify that all safety equipment is aboard and working correctly. Once underway, drivers must be alert to prevent accidents and to drive their trucks efficiently. At the end of each run, they are required by the U.S. Department of Transportation to complete reports about the trip and the condition of the truck and to give a detailed report of any accident.

PREPARATION FOR BECOMING A TRUCK DRIVER

Drivers must meet the qualifications and standards set by both federal and state regulations. Minimum qualifications include being at least twenty-one years old if they will be engaged in interstate commerce, passing a physical examination, having good hearing, having 20/40 vision with or without correction for each eye, and having normal blood pressure. All drivers of trucks that carry at least twenty-six thousand pounds (which includes most long-distance trucks) need to obtain a special commercial driver's license from the state in which they live. Also, drivers must pass periodic random tests for drug and alcohol use. Both states and trucking companies often have higher standards than the ones described here.

To obtain a commercial driver's license as well as learn how to drive trucks, most long-distance drivers attend tractor-trailer driver training programs at private and public technical vocational schools. Drivers should select schools that have been certified by the Professional Truck Driver Institute of America and that have been approved by prospective employers. A list of certified programs as well as the booklet *Careers in Trucking* can be obtained by writing the Professional Truck Driver Institute of America, 2200 Mill Road, Alexandria, VA 22314, or by visiting the organization's website at ptdi.org.

SALARY, BENEFITS, AND ADVANCEMENT

Long-distance tractor-trailers drivers average $42,000 per year. However, experienced drivers can earn from $45,000 to $60,000 or more. Company drivers receive standard benefits. Some long-distance drivers advance by purchasing a truck and going into business for themselves. A few may advance to dispatcher, to manager, or to traffic work.

THE FUTURE

Job opportunities for truck drivers vary from year to year because the amount of freight moved by trucks fluctuates with the economy. Increased use of rail, air, and ship transportation will require more truck drivers to pick up and deliver shipments. Demand for long-distance drivers should also remain strong because they transport perishable and time-sensitive goods more efficiently than other forms of transportation. And numerous job openings will occur as drivers leave this field. Because this job does not require education beyond high school, competition is expected for the jobs with the most attractive earnings and working conditions.

LOOKING AT A JOB AS A TRAVEL PHOTOGRAPHER

Travel photographers take pictures for magazines that feature travel, exotic lands, and wildlife, such as *National Geographic* and *Travel & Leisure*. They also take pictures that are used in newspapers, calendars, books, greeting cards, tour company brochures, and advertisements. Many photographers work for stock houses—agencies that have libraries of thousands of slides that are sold to publications and organizations.

This is a very competitive occupation, and pay is low. Most travel photographers are freelancers who devote a great deal of their time to soliciting jobs and to selling the work that they have done. However, they also truly have the opportunity to travel.

LOOKING AT A JOB AS A TRAVEL WRITER

Being a travel writer is decidedly one job that involves a great amount of travel—some writers travel as much as 70 to 80 percent of the time. Travel writing jobs can be found on the staffs of newspapers, consumer-oriented travel magazines, and travel trade publications. There are also jobs writing and updating travel books; more than one thousand new guidebooks are published each year. Travel writing jobs are also available in radio, television, and cable television as well as with tour companies, lecture series, tourist offices, and wherever a need for written travel information exists.

Pay can be good for travel writers; however, job competition is fierce. Jobs at newspapers and magazines are limited, and these publications want to hire experienced travel writers. Guidebook publishers also want experienced travel authors. Generally, travel writers need to establish their credibility by writing travel articles and having them published in a local newspaper or a small trade publication. They will usually find it easier to get an initial job with a trade publication writing about what is happening in the travel industry than with a consumer magazine writing about exotic locales around the world.

Many travel writers opt to become freelancers, which means constantly finding a market for one's writing. However, by changing a travel article to fit different audiences, the same basic material can be sold to several publications.

FOR MORE INFORMATION

There are many other travel careers that may appeal to travel lovers, such as careers with the merchant marine, tour operators, and car rental companies, to name just a few. For more information on travel careers, read *Opportunities in Travel Careers* by Robert Scott Milne (McGraw-Hill), *Careers for Travel Buffs and Other Restless Types* by Paul Plawin (McGraw-Hill), and *Inside Secrets to Finding a Career in Travel* by Karen Rubin (Jist Publishing).

7

CAREERS AT TOUR COMPANIES AS A GUIDE AND IN OTHER JOBS

Sightseeing, special-interest, convention, and many other tours are now operated worldwide by tour companies. These companies are found in nearly every town and city across the United States and vary in size from owner-operated to having employees in several departments, such as guiding and sales and marketing. Tour companies may package and sell trips wholesale to smaller travel planning companies, associations, meeting planners, or businesses seeking trips as employee bonuses. Other tour companies sell directly to consumers. Tour packages include transportation, accommodations, and sightseeing.

LOOKING AT TOUR TRAVEL OPTIONS

The means of travel for tours range from bus, ship, train, or plane to any combination. Tours may be local, perhaps even within the geographic location of the tour company, or they can be long distances.

Buses and Planes

Buses are a popular choice for transportation for both local and long-distance tours because bus travel can be very affordable and passengers can stop at many points along the bus tour. A local tour can last for a partial day or full day of travel and bring a group through a historic area of a city, to a nearby attraction, or to community festival.

Plane travel allows people to take getaways, or short excursions of a day or two, to more-distant locations. Tropical climates offer great appeal for winter-weary individuals, as do ski trips to the mountains for Sunbelt residents. These trips have become very popular because leisure-time opportunities are limited for some individuals. The overall cost of getaways is greater than bus or car travel, but some travelers are willing to pay more for the convenience.

Tours of greater distances typically last several days to several weeks and frequently use multiple modes of transportation. For instance, a plane may transport a group to Europe. Once on that continent, though, the travelers may use bus or rail travel to move from country to country.

Rail Excursions

Although not as popular today as it once was, rail travel for special private lines, such as tours through the Copper Canyon of Mexico, sell very well. Travelers are treated to such features as oversized windows, reclining seats with ample leg room, full bar and dining service cars, and lounge cars. While winding through scenic territories, tour participants experience breathtaking views. A tour company then provides overnight stays at hotels along the rail line and side visits to cultural and historic sites.

Other types of rail tours that have been popular in recent years are wine train tours and mystery train tours. These special-interest tours attract clients with their unique themes and mode of transportation.

Cruises

Cruises may last from three days to as long as several weeks. Guests appreciate the chance to have a wide variety of experiences on board, such as incredibly fine dining, multiple amenities (like massages and physical conditioning), sport activities, entertainment, and gaming. Many cruise lines have now purchased their own islands to offer the travelers opportunities to relax on private beaches, swim, snorkel, and scuba dive. And the port calls made by the ships are a prime feature, with special land tour packages to help guests see as much as possible when docked.

Some tour travelers desire a more intimate or unique way to travel than the large cruise ships. The paddle boats that cruise the rivers of the United States offer such appeal, as do the tall ships that elegantly set sail. Smaller vessels are also available; for example, passenger boats may transport only one hundred passengers and cruise through the pristine waters off the coast of Alaska. Depending on the destination, these smaller cruises may be as short as one day.

TOUR SETTINGS

Destination choices for tours range from anywhere in the United States to anywhere in the world. The sites visited may be historic, educational, theme related, natural wonders or natural beauty, competition related, exotic, cosmopolitan, rural, artistic, and/or cultural.

Historic sites have always been and will continue to be attractive settings for tour companies. Customers wish to see places that they have read about, and the tour company may select sites that have been a key part of American history. Theme tours are also perennial favorites, such as a trip to Branson, Missouri, that permits tour customers to attend their favorite country singer's performance.

Many sports fans request trips organized with lodging and tickets to special athletic events. The Super Bowl, World Series, Master's Golf Tournament, and U.S. Open Tennis Tournament are popular tour choices. Fans also join tours to follow their favorite teams to play-offs. And in Olympics years, many different tours make it easy to see the events.

Cosmopolitan settings, such as New York City and Chicago, offer multiple attractions for tours. "Big city" Christmas shopping trips are one-day or weekend shopping excursions that allow tour participants to "shop 'til they drop," and attend theater or concert events.

LOOKING AT A CAREER AS A TOUR GUIDE

Guiding tours is a good introductory position with a tour operations company. The primary task of the guide is to ensure that the trip occurs as planned. This means being responsible for guest safety; providing an interesting experience; organizing the daily itinerary; handling all problems; alleviating emergency situations; interacting with suppliers; giving narratives about sites; and completing daily reports about the activities, meals, and accommodations. A guide is also responsible for keeping a trip on its daily schedule; organizing the customers during transit and when stopped for touring, dining, or sleeping; assisting with customers' special needs; resolving daily problems; educating the customers about the sites being visited; and entertaining them whenever needed.

A guide is a cross between a babysitter and a leader, educator, negotiator, problem solver, and entertainer. These diverse activities and responsibilities can be very demanding. Typically, the guide is the first one to rise in the morning and the last one to go to bed in the evening.

On an international tour, the tour operator may hire locals to serve as guides. Local guides can give tremendous insights into the people, their customs, and their culture as well as providing safety dos and don'ts; help with language barriers; and assistance with money equivalencies, exchange rates, and exchange procedures.

RESPONSIBILITIES

Tour guides' main goal is for every customer to be happy with the trip. To fulfill this goal, they typically work twelve to fourteen hours per day. They start each day, each activity, each change in location with one thought: "Did I double-check—even triple-check—each detail of the trip?"

In the morning, the tour guide checks the breakfast service for readiness at least one hour before guests on the tour are to eat. At breakfast, the guide greets travelers and reviews the itinerary for the day. Then the guide checks at the hotel front desk to verify that checkout procedures are completed. The guide also confirms with the bus driver that everyone's luggage has been loaded and the departure time and route for the day. Calling ahead to the day's destination sites, lunch stops, and lodging for the evening is also done at this time.

When the guests are seated on the bus, the guide reviews the day's activities and answers any questions and concerns. To help the travelers learn about the next destination, the tour guide will have information available about the site. Upon arrival, the guide may simply "turn the guests over to the site" or may escort them around the site. Either way, time management is the guide's top priority.

Once the day's activities, which may include other stops, are completed, the top priority for the guide and guests is getting to the hotel. Once there, room assignments are checked and, if needed, dinner or evening snacks take place. The guide previews the next day of activities for the group and makes sure everyone gets settled. The guide then completes all of the paperwork required by the tour company and reviews the next day's responsibilities.

PREPARATION FOR A CAREER AS A TOUR GUIDE

Training is usually on the job so that tour guides can learn the procedures and policies of their employer through observation. This training might consist of taking several trips with an experienced guide to assist in all of the responsibilities required to keep a group moving through the schedule. Training also includes education on the destination sites or attractions. Guides are taught about common pitfalls of this profession, as handling people is very demanding. For example, some individuals want constant attention; training provides appropriate solutions to pacify a demanding guest without sacrificing attention to the other customers. Some schools also have short courses designed for prospective guides.

SPECIAL ATTRIBUTES OF A TOUR GUIDE

Qualifications include being a "people person," being good with oral and written communications, being an entertainer, being able to resolve problems, and being able to handle a crisis. Tour guides need to be knowledgeable about reading maps and meticulous in handling details. A degree credential is advantageous, but so, too, are decision-making skills, multicultural skills, and organizing skills, which can be learned in other work experiences. Part-time or full-time work experiences in other types of hospitality businesses, such as restaurants or hotels, offer useful exposure in these areas. Physically, tour guides must have an excellent stamina level to work the long days required while on tour. Fitness is essential to coping well with the challenges and stresses of guiding tours.

SALARY AND BENEFITS

Travel tour guides receive wages of approximately $100 per day, plus a meal allowance, but these wages depend upon the complexity of the trip. Unusually large groups, tours made up of travelers with special requirements (disabled travelers), particularly long trips, or a large number of activities can lead to higher daily rates. While tipping is not expected, extremely pleased guests give a gratuity to the guide as a thank-you, which can increase annual income. Guides who work in establishments such as historical homes and as hunting, fishing, and mountain-climbing guides typically earn between minimum wage and slightly more than $10 per hour, depending upon their experience. Some also receive tips.

Companies offer free trips to destinations to establish itineraries or prepare an inaugural trip to a new location, which is an excellent benefit. Guides who work full-time year-round receive such benefits as life insurance, health insurance, and retirement programs.

PERKS AND PRESSURES OF BEING A TOUR GUIDE

Tour guides frequently cite the opportunity to see new places as the greatest advantage of this career choice. If the company is involved in international tours, visiting foreign countries is an attractive possibility. Each trip also offers the opportunity to meet new people who vary widely in their interests, backgrounds, and ages. And whether the trip is one day or several weeks in length, a special bond develops between the guide and the group members as they share in the excitement of the trip.

As very popular trips are repeated annually or even more frequently, the contact people at the attraction sites and lodging properties can become close working associates. With each tour, the guides and the employees of other businesses can pool their efforts to make certain that the travelers have the best possible experience—a "win-win-win" situation.

With the diversity of clients on a tour, however, guides are challenged to please all of their customers all of the time. The purchasers of a tour package generally represent some degree of differences in economic, social, geographical, cultural, educational, and age backgrounds, and tour guides must address these differences effectively.

Another challenge for tour guides is maintaining good spirits among all of the clients. Traveling and touring can be tiresome for the customers. When nerves become frayed, the guide must work to bring harmony and humor to the group. Another drawback to tour guiding is that some tour-planning businesses do not frequently change destinations, but guides cannot reveal their boredom to the customers.

Finally, problems do occur despite the best planning efforts to ensure a perfect tour. A guide is responsible for using contingency planning to handle problems and provide guest satisfaction through the chosen resolutions. Contingency planning requires examining the problem and all possible solutions within company policies and procedures to find the solution that best fits the situation.

THE PERSONAL STORY OF A TOUR GUIDE

Like many tour guides, Whitney Stull works in a travel office when she is not serving as a guide. Her employer is the alumni association of a major university that offers approximately fifty-five educational tours each year. With experience as a campus guide, a love of people, and solid organizational skills as well as a burning desire to travel internationally, Whitney knew a job in the travel industry was the right one for her. She found her job through a posting on the university's website.

Long before a tour begins, Whitney spends considerable time preparing for the trip. She spends several hours with the tour planner discussing exactly what each day on the tour will look like. No matter how well the days are outlined, Whitney has to be flexible on the road and quickly think of solutions to problems from the delay of a charter flight to a major earthquake. She must also think through the financial side of the tour. First, she needs to know the exchange rate for each country. Then she must plan how much money to carry to pay local guides and bus drivers and to tip porters, waitstaff, and maids. Another pretrip essential is become familiar with the people on the tour. Whitney needs to know their birthdays, medical conditions, and special interests. She memorizes the names of the participants and makes sure that she has their passport numbers and emergency contact information. Her pretrip preparation is not done until she has learned as much as she can about the places that the tour will visit.

The university tours use local guides and lecturers from the school, so Whitney does not have these responsibilities. However, she has the responsibility of coordinating the activities of these people to make the best possible tour. While preparation makes most days go smoothly, there are almost always some minor glitches. It is not unusual for Whitney to have to help someone find a lost passport, reschedule an activity because of an unexpected traffic jam, or give an impromptu speech on behalf of the group. Whitney advises prospective tour guides to get experience that develops the organizational and people skills needed for this job. And once they have a job like hers, she encourages them to develop an appreciation of the different cultures that they encounter.

LOOKING AT A CAREER AS A TOUR PLANNER

Large tour operators, whether they sell wholesale or retail, have employees who plan the trips. Small operators plan the trips that they offer, then sell the trip to organizations and individuals, and even serve as tour guide. Planners research the popularity and demand for specific sites, investigate all costs, negotiate prices, establish travel dates and times, and coordinate with other companies whose services might be needed for transportation, lodging, food, or entertainment.

The planning and sales of a tour depend upon knowing the customers' demographics: age, income, and interests. It is very important to organize trips that appeal to customers' particular interests. Planners must also be aware of quality businesses that can be used as part of the trip. A destination trip can nearly be ruined, for example, if the planner selects a restaurant that is understaffed, overpriced for the quality, or unclean. The tour planner's rewards are found in the satisfaction of planning and overseeing the execution of a flawless tour.

As part of the research for destination selection, tour planners may visit the sites under consideration. This gives the tour planner a firsthand experience in a country, state, or city to see the special attractions and to evaluate the food and lodging facilities.

THE PERSONAL STORY OF A TOUR PLANNER

Besides working as a tour guide, Whitney Stull works in the alumni travel office of her university on the planning and coordinating of trips. The actual day-to-day, hour-by-hour plans are made by tour planners at both large and small companies. Whitney then checks the plans to make sure that the hotels and restaurants are in the right location and of the quality the travel office clients want. She checks that a day is not overloaded with activities and does not involve too much time on buses. Whitney uses feedback from clients who have made previous trips to the same location to ensure that a trip is right for the type of travelers who make trips with her organization. Whitney then goes back to the trip planner with any changes that need to be made.

Whitney is also responsible for marketing trips. This involves writing copy and working with brochure designers as well as doing all the budgeting to determine the cost of the trip. Her job responsibilities extend to working with the trip lecturers on the topics that will be discussed and planning special events. Before her work on a trip is done, Whitney also prepares all of the predeparture information for the travelers.

LOOKING AT OTHER CAREERS IN TOUR OPERATIONS

Reservationists have the first contact with customers, so they must be pleasant and skilled at determining their interests. Eliciting information about customers' interests is necessary so that the customers can receive marketing information that will help sell a tour. The sales staff follows up on all customer contacts, hoping to turn each lead into a booking. Both reservationists and sales staff are rewarded for the quality and quantity of their selling.

Tour companies of substantial size also employ people to promote and advertise the tours. Advertising can be done through brochures, which the salespeople might design in conjunction with the planners. With word processing software, salespeople do much of their own creative work for advertising. The sales staff must also stay current with new trends in marketing, such as using the Internet to feature their company and its trips. If they work for a wholesale company, the sales staff may visit key sites or attend marketplace meetings to feature their planned activities and get leads on bookings. Similarly, sales staffs with retail tour companies determine the advertising media to use and set up general travel seminars that are free to the public. After bookings are made, the sales staff oversees confirmation of deposits. They also send out all needed information on the tour—information on climate, weather, and appropriate clothing; travel requirements, such as birth certificate or passport; and pertinent materials about the destinations.

Large tour companies employ people to provide support services in the accounting and human resources departments. Accounting employees help with the financial records of the company. They oversee deposits and final payments for tours and check disbursements for services used at hotels, restaurants, and tour sites. Human resources handles payroll records and benefit packages.

Employees of small tour companies wear many hats. Their positions include planning, marketing, selling, and escorting. The incredible variety of tasks performed by the owner/employee of a small tour operation company makes it necessary for this individual to be highly organized, very detail oriented, quick thinking, excellent at decision making, and personable with customers.

PREPARATION FOR A CAREER IN TOUR OPERATIONS

To work in tour guiding, planning, and/or sales, educational requirements include a minimum of a high school education. Courses in communications and business management are helpful in establishing knowledge and skills in dealing with people and completing paperwork. Membership in student organizations and holding a leadership role as officer or committee chair is valuable to help learn organizational and leadership skills. Clubs such as Distributive Education Clubs of America (DECA) and Future Homemakers Association/Home Economics-Related Occupations (FHA/HERO) are excellent choices. Both offer opportunities to participate in contests that demand problem solving and people skills, in addition to offering the obvious leadership development positions of holding an office. Managing a sports team is another way to obtain some job-related preparation. Teams travel, and they need help packing equipment and supplies for their trips.

Larger tour companies or companies specializing in itineraries with international or educational settings may require a two- or four-year college degree. Preferred majors are tourism and hospitality management, with their emphasis on business management, service management, and food and lodging operations. To complement a hospitality degree, a minor in liberal arts, especially foreign languages, history, or sociology, is an excellent choice. Computer courses, as a minor, are another excellent complement to a hospitality major, for skills in promoting and selling the trips and for record keeping. A communications degree is also beneficial as a major or minor because good communication is essential in every part of the tourist industry. A major or minor in marketing or accounting can help prepare the tour operator with strategies to sell the trips and to assure financial profitability.

Some professional organizations offer a variety of programs that can give further credentials to a tour operations employee. A Certified Travel Counselor (CTC) designation is granted by the Institute of Certified Travel Agents. The National Tour Foundation has a program for Certified Tour Professional (CTP). A Certified Travel Industry Specialist (CTIS) is a certificate program available through the American Bus Association.

SALARY AND BENEFITS

Benefits such as life insurance, medical benefits, paid days off, and/or retirement programs vary widely in availability depending on the size of the tour operation company and the number of full-time employees. Since many tour operation companies use a small skeleton staff of full-time employees to plan, organize, and sell trips, benefit packages are not too common. Full-time employees in planning, sales, or support areas typically earn salaries under $30,000. However, experienced trip planners may make more than $50,000 at larger companies. People who own tour operation companies generally have much greater incomes than their employees. It would appear that the potential to earn a liberal income is unlimited.

LOOKING AT OTHER JOBS IN TOURS

Destination management companies have a "one-stop shopping" philosophy of business. These businesses have expanded on the tour business by not only planning and executing tours but selling other types of services to the customer, too. For example, if an association is planning its annual convention, the members might want tours, entertainment, program speakers, food and lodging arrangements, and airport meet-and-greet services, among other possible services.

The destination management company is hired to provide all of the services for the customer. As the intermediary, the destination management company listens to the wishes of the customers and then arranges for the activities they have selected. The destination management company saves customers time and energy by completing all of the details for a group's choices of activities.

To work for a destination management company, the required skills are to be patient with people; to inform customers of what is really involved in each activity; to advise customers on the time, cost, and overall quality of possible activities; to be credible by delivering the quality that is expected; and to be respectful of the other businesses whose services you contract. Destination management companies are finding a growing market for their services because customers like working with a single business to make all necessary arrangements.

THE FUTURE

Tour companies are stable, with modest growth in the past decade. However, operators are particularly susceptible to changes in the economy. Local, national, or international economic variances may affect individuals' and companies' discretionary spending. When the economy is in a slowdown period, people and organizations delay trips.

FOR MORE INFORMATION

For more information, visit local tour operations companies and interview tour escorts, planners, and sales staff. The National Tourism Foundation, at ntfonline.org, has a wealth of materials available regarding courses, internships, and colleges and universities that offer tourism courses and/or degrees (see Appendix C).

C H A P T E R

8

CAREERS AT AMUSEMENT PARKS

The single largest amusement park is Disney World in Florida; the Magic Kingdom has more than fifteen million visitors annually. Beyond this colossus, parks are found all around the country in various sizes from Valleyfair in Minnesota, the largest park in the Upper Midwest, to the small water parks in many communities. No matter how large or small amusement parks are, the guests are happy, relaxed, and excited. Coupled with this carefree attitude of the customer is the wide array of rides that appeal to guests of all ages. Many amusement parks have various sizes and shapes of roller coasters and other breathtaking attractions to excite visitors. The employees' jobs are made easier because guests have selected a park to experience these thrills. A major benefit of working in an amusement park is serving guests who are interested in having a good time.

The same is true for parks with a greater emphasis on show entertainment. Visitors to such places as Dollywood in Tennessee and the SeaWorld parks have high levels of anticipation for the shows featuring "stars," from the country and western singers of Dollywood to a killer whale and dolphins at SeaWorld.

SETTINGS OF AMUSEMENT PARKS

Very large parks have multiple separate areas within the park complex. For example, Disney World includes the Magic Kingdom, Epcot, MGM, Animal Kingdom, Blizzard Beach, and Typhoon Lagoon. The Disney Institute merges entertainment and personal enrichment; guests can learn about animation, culinary arts, photography, storytelling, show business, landscape design, and interior design or choose fitness and lifestyle classes.

Smaller amusement parks, such as Holiday World and Splashing Safari in Santa Claus, Indiana, offer traditional rides, entertainment, and water rides. Other amusement parks have down-home appeal, such as Bonfante Gardens in Gilroy, California, which combines four unique gardens and amusement rides with the mid-twentieth-century history and agricultural roots of the area.

Universal Studios originally selected a setting of television and major motion picture–making to attract visitors. With opportunities to see and participate in major motion picture technology, guests learn and have fun at the same time. Ride attractions such as Back to the Future, Jurassic Park, and Revenge of the Mummy frequently have long lines of riders waiting to have an experience that simulates the action of the movie.

Water parks use slides, fountains, rivers, and pools to appeal to guests. Water activities are enjoyed by people of all ages, so these parks have an enormous appeal. They may operate independently from any other park or may be a facility within a larger amusement-park complex.

Other settings of amusement parks focus on activities other than rides. The SeaWorld parks have an in-depth representation of ocean life. Customers are attracted to the educational aspect of the park and are given the opportunity to be up close to ocean creatures. Another interest area for amusement parks is the inclusion of wild game areas, where the animals can roam freely. People are fascinated by exotic creatures, and guests are moved through the wild game area on a tram or bus to observe the animals in a natural setting.

LOOKING AT JOBS IN AMUSEMENT PARKS

Amusement parks have many departments to provide their services and products to customers. From entry-level positions through management levels, these departments are staffed with tens to hundreds to even thousands of employees. Jobs at parks are typically found in these departments: food preparation and service, attractions operations and maintenance, transportation and parking, guest services, groundskeeping, entertainment, wardrobe, laundry, and lodging services. There may also be other departments, depending on the types of attractions and the amenities offered at the park. For every position in every department, the most important responsibility is to be friendly to the amusement-park guests.

Ride Operations

Large numbers of entry-level employees are employed in attractions operations. Ride operators have many responsibilities. Amusement parks frequently use rides as the prime marketing tool to attract visitors, and ride operators must support that promotion. Major thrill rides such as roller coasters, where speed, hills, and turns offer elements of excitement and adventure, require the operators to build up this mood through their interactions and communications with guests.

It is also very important that ride operators have full knowledge of the safety requirements for guests using a ride. Some rides are not safe for individuals who have heart conditions, motion sickness, or back problems. Pregnant women may not ride on some rides, and young children may also be hurt on certain rides. Therefore, ride operators must carefully screen all riders to see that no one who would be at risk gets on the ride. This requires tact and diplomacy to help direct customers to make another choice for a ride, especially with young children who want to enjoy the most thrilling rides in the park.

Another responsibility is the correct operation of the ride. Guests must enter and exit the ride without risking injury, and ride operators oversee this activity. Equipment checks must be made regularly to ensure that there are no problems. Severe weather changes may affect the safety of operating a ride. Ride operators are required to report any condition that might affect the safe operation of a ride and to close the ride if their supervisor instructs them to do so.

Ride narratives may also be performed by the employees in ride operations. For rides that simulate an underwater dive or an earthquake, for example, the narration sets the scene for the guests, builds their level of anticipation, and makes them feel the total experience of the ride. For each group that boards these rides, the operators give the same basic "acting" performances.

Ride Maintenance

Sharing responsibility for the operation of rides are the employees of the maintenance and repair department. Personnel in this department conduct regular inspections of seats, harnesses, belts, tracks, doors, and latches as well as the entrance and exit areas of attractions to make sure that everything is in good working order. Any possible deficiency for safe operating is listed on a work order. The priority is to continue the operation of the ride safely, so all maintenance possible is done on a prevention basis—that is, before a minor difficulty becomes a genuine hazard. However, sometimes repairs must be made in emergency situations during peak business times, and employees must respond quickly to make the appropriate repairs. If repairs cannot be made within a short time, then maintenance workers report to their supervisors so that decisions can be made to close a ride for part or all of a day.

Water/Pool Recreation Areas

Water activities play an important role in most theme parks. On hot summer days, the water attractions of a park are filled with crowds of people. Pools, streams, slides, and sprays are all fun activities for customers, whether they participate or watch. Boating, skiing, jet-skiing, sailing, canoeing, and paddle-boating also appeal to guests. Employees' responsibilities in water/pool recreation departments are to provide for the safety of the guests, oversee the number of guests using a water space or floating device, train guests on the safe operation of equipment, and check equipment for operating safety. These employees must be able to perform water rescue and administer cardiopulmonary resuscitation (CPR).

Park Maintenance

General maintenance of an entire park offers various positions in painting, air-conditioning and refrigeration, carpentry, masonry, electrical and mechanical systems, pest control, plumbing, and audiovisual technology. Employees in these areas provide preventive checks on all types of equipment, fixtures, and furnishings in the park. Their primary responsibility is to keep the park looking clean and new by having everything in good working order. Another key function of maintenance work is to provide safety for guests. Any accident that occurs due to a broken piece of equipment or a fixture could be a major liability to the park.

Retail and Food Outlets

Surrounding the rides are an assortment of gift and souvenir shops, food and beverage stands, restaurants, and carnival stands for game playing. These areas are always located near premier rides, because they offer diversions to guests waiting to get on a ride and activities to occupy guests who are waiting for friends and relatives to complete a ride. Employees in these departments need good customer skills to promote interest in eating, shopping, browsing, relaxing, or game playing and to make customers content while they wait. Employees also order stock, complete inventories, prevent shoplifting, keep accurate sales records, and control cash.

Entertainment

Many amusement parks have a substantial number of entertainment attractions. These programs focus on quick-movement, high-energy shows that please everyone in a crowd. The entertainers must be musically and athletically talented, personable, and able to get and keep the spectators' attention. Entertainment is not typically the focus of the amusement park; rather, it is an opportunity for park attendees to relax and rest from the thrills of the rides. By having a type of "quiet time" activity within the park, the park can increase the length of time visitors stay. Entertainers sing and dance, tell jokes, and solicit involvement from the audience. Audience participation brings guests in, so interactive themes for the shows are very common.

Some amusement parks have characters who provide entertainment by mingling with the guests. These characters meet and greet the customers, pose for photographs, and promote the friendliness of the park. As a member of the cast of characters, contact with the guests is constant. While they are entertaining, the characters must let all guests know that they are special and give them a few seconds of their time. They often do this using only nonverbal communication, which makes these positions extremely demanding and requires very creative and patient employees. Another challenge that occurs for the well-known costumed characters, like Mickey Mouse, is crowd control. The popularity of some characters is so great that excessive crowds quickly form. These characters must keep moving without appearing to slight any fan. Frequently, one or two security personnel accompany the most popular characters to ensure safety of the character and the park guests.

A primary feature of SeaWorld's entertainment is to have the mammals perform for the guests. Killer whale shows and dolphin shows are very popular. The entertainment depends on individuals who are talented and personable, but who are also trained in sea life. These employees are responsible for training the animals and for their care. Since the mammals are captive, they receive routine exams to ensure their health.

Water shows with skiing tricks and boat maneuvers also entertain the guests at amusement parks. Employees in these shows must be talented in the use of different types of skis and be able to perform acrobatic stunts, such as jumps and twists and the formation of human pyramids or chains.

Wardrobe

All members of the entertainment department and all employees in ride operations and retail outlets have special costume wardrobes that must be maintained. Keeping the costumes cleaned, repaired, and inventoried requires a large department of employees. Laundry, pressing, and alterations are typical tasks performed by wardrobe. These employees may also design and construct new uniforms to meet the needs of new rides or retail stores opening within a park.

Transportation and Parking Services

Employees of the transportation and parking department must get thousands of vehicles and the occupants of those vehicles into and out of the park. These employees may be assigned to direct parking in the guest lots or to operate shuttles from the lots to the park. Their most important responsibility is traffic flow. Whether people are on wheels or on foot, traffic must move in a safe and efficient manner. This is especially true for young children entering the park, as their anticipation and eagerness may contribute to impulsive movements that endanger their safety.

Special attention is also paid to disabled guests. Obtaining wheelchairs or motorized carts helps these guests feel welcome and allows them to enjoy the park. Transportation employees need to assist these guests in an appropriate manner. Counting entries to the park, giving directions, and answering general questions about the park's operations are other tasks commonly performed by the individuals in the transportation department.

Security

While they are on the park grounds, guests want to know that they are in a safe environment. Employees in the security department provide for every possible aspect of customer safety, including locating missing children or missing parents, watching out for shoplifters and pickpockets, and being highly visible to deter any individual who might have illegal activities planned. This final task is very critical around the food vendors, the retail outlets, and the admissions gates because these are where cash is spent.

Support Services

Behind the scenes at amusement parks are the support service personnel of the reservations, clerical, human resources, and accounting departments. Individuals who work in these departments have a variety of tasks. Reservationists complete forms necessary to reserve spaces and communicate to the supervisors in operations. Knowledge of big groups or special groups that may be attending the park that day, such as a senior citizens' group, helps operations employees prepare to perform their jobs.

Clerical positions require speed and accuracy in keyboarding and other computer skills, with an excellent command of grammar, punctuation, and spelling. Other requirements include strong oral communications skills, excellent organization skills, and attention to detail. Furthermore, these employees must be able to maintain the confidentiality of records and prepared reports, as these documents may pertain to the proprietary nature of the park or to personnel files.

Accounting department employees compile the costs for each area of the park's operations and compare them to the sales generated by the park. Their results are used by management to determine which rides and venues are operating efficiently and to determine ways to improve less profitable attractions.

The staff in human resources determines staff needs in operations and support services, recruits potential employees, collects and reviews applications, conducts interviews, provides orientation to new hires, and documents performance by keeping thorough and accurate records on all personnel.

Recruiting potential employees is a challenge for most parks, but especially so for the parks with seasonal positions. Human resources employees use creative means to discover possible employees, such as recruiting college students, high school students, stay-at-home moms, and retired people.

Other support departments that are critical to the overall success of the park include marketing, group sales, development, and construction. The key role for employees in marketing is to determine the groups that should be targeted for advertising campaigns so as to increase the number of visitors. Group sales personnel work with associations and businesses that want to bring in a large group of people. Sales employees help plan the budgets and activities for the big groups, ensuring that these groups enjoy as much of the park as possible.

Employees in the development department create ideas for new attractions. New concepts must be continually researched to give the park a competitive edge as an attraction. As population demographics change, the development staff works with the marketing staff to keep a balance of activity choices to appeal to all guests.

Amusement parks use construction departments to build or remodel the park as designed by the development department. Cost-efficiency and construction schedules are important responsibilities because many parks are in continuous or near-continuous operation, and construction areas must be carefully secured to prevent accidents. Guests must be moved around the construction with as little inconvenience as possible so that the park maintains its traffic flow and customers.

Internships

College students can learn more about the amusement-park industry by becoming an intern. Most internships are paid positions. Internships are available at many parks throughout the United States. Participants typically work from thirty to forty hours per week.

WORKING CONDITIONS

Very large amusement parks offer year-round employment, which is an advantage for employees. Some amusement parks offer extended seasons, operating on a full-time basis from late spring through early fall. These parks may be open on weekends in late fall and early spring, but the parks are closed in the winter months. Some parks reopen in November and December for the holiday season on a part-time or full-time basis because guests enjoy shopping and viewing the decorative splendor. Closure for several months does present an employment disadvantage for amusement-park workers. Most of these workers must find another job on a temporary basis or consider the park job as a second job.

Jobs in amusement parks offer considerable flexibility in working hours. Many parks have a seven-day workweek and operating hours of 9:00 A.M. through midnight. Employees can plan a work schedule that allows them to attend to other activities, such as school schedules or other employment situations. With the tremendous range of hours, personal preferences like those of the late sleeper or early riser can be accommodated.

Amusement parks generally have very precise codes governing the dress and appearance of all employees. Grooming requirements usually include guidelines on hair length and arrangement, hands and fingernails, and facial hair as well as governing the wearing of jewelry and the exposing of body tattoos.

PREPARATION FOR BECOMING AN AMUSEMENT-PARK EMPLOYEE

Many of the entry-level positions at amusement parks are filled by students attending high school. Employees as young as fifteen years old may be able to work in food service. Sixteen is usually the minimum age for the admissions, retail, ride operations, entertainment, and wardrobe departments. To work in the areas of cash control and guest relations, employees must often be eighteen years old, while security positions typically require employees to be twenty-one.

To be employed at amusement parks, young employees must demonstrate through their high school activities, grades, and attendance that they are outgoing, motivated, and responsible. The parks value participation in school or community groups or on athletic teams because this can indicate an ability to work with others as a team member.

High school courses in communications, foreign languages, and business management are good selections because these courses will help students learn about people and about business operations. It is also important to have a solid attendance record, as employers look at these records as measures of maturity and responsibility. Previous work experience in any type of hospitality industry (food service, lodging, clubs, or concessions) is valuable because these positions require development of customer contact skills.

To work in supervisory positions in the various departments or in semi-skilled positions, employees must have a high school diploma and some type of postsecondary training. For positions in the maintenance department, a technical school certificate or a degree from an associate or baccalaureate institution is needed to work in electrical, mechanical, or air-conditioning and refrigeration jobs. For positions in departments such as development and design, computer software and hardware expertise and a college degree are required to use computer-aided design (CAD). For customer service positions in retail or in hospitality departments, a certificate, an associate's degree, or a bachelor's degree in food service and lodging management, culinary arts, or business management may be needed.

Training for all entry-level positions at amusement parks typically begins with videos and workshops to teach new employees the responsibilities of their jobs and to train them in customer interaction. Then on-the-job training begins in the area where the new employee will work. Since customer service is the most important aspect of every employee's job, the parks emphasize and reemphasize the importance of working with guests in a warm, friendly way.

SPECIAL ATTRIBUTES OF AN AMUSEMENT-PARK EMPLOYEE

Amusement-park employees will be happy in their work if they genuinely like people. Because park employees must interact with guests of different backgrounds, they need to be good at communicating, patient, and positive. With the international appeal that all amusement parks have, all employees need to be able to relate to people from many cultures.

ADVANCEMENT

One advantage of working for a large amusement park is the opportunity to move laterally or vertically in job positions. With thousands of employees, employees can make many moves to other departments or to other parts of the park. This provides variety in the employment opportunities with the park, helps to cross-train employees, and serves as a means of preparing outstanding employees to move into supervisory or management positions.

SALARY AND BENEFITS

Entry-level positions in amusement parks may begin at minimum wage. However, hourly wages for entry-level jobs in areas where the employment rate is high may be substantially above minimum wage. In general, earnings are low in amusement parks, reflecting the large number of part-time and seasonal jobs. Positions requiring some training, education, skills, previous work experience, and/or credentials, such as lifeguards, reservationists, maintenance workers, culinary assistants, and security personnel, can pay higher wages. The average hourly wage for maintenance workers is more than $10 per hour, while security workers earn more than $9. Employees in food operations can earn between $7 and $10 per hour. Skilled positions in such departments as accounting, marketing, and sales may start at $9 to $10 per hour. At some parks, besides hourly pay, it is possible to earn bonuses of as much as a dollar extra for every hour worked by fulfilling an employment contract. In areas with labor shortages, employees may also earn bonuses for referring people who are subsequently hired.

Benefits typically include medical, dental, and life insurance for full-time employees. Depending on the size of the park, part-time employees may have some of these benefits, too. Overtime hours may be offered at time-and-a-half rates. Employees receive free admission to the park, and many parks provide guest passes when a minimum number of hours have been worked with a corresponding level of competency. Employees get free parking, and their uniforms and their maintenance are provided. Parks also offer their employees discounts at the retail stores. Some parks even offer on-site housing at a nominal cost or provide a housing subsidy.

PERKS AND PRESSURES OF BEING AN AMUSEMENT-PARK EMPLOYEE

Amusement parks offer employment in a fun-filled, high-energy environment. Customers of all ages laugh, scream, and squeal with delight, and they appreciate the part that each employee plays in their fun. Interaction with guests is very satisfying.

Working for an amusement park means working as a member of a team or family. Managers treat employees with respect because they know that the employees have the responsibility of meeting the customers' expectations. And working together is satisfying for amusement-park employees. Cross-training is also rewarding, as employees develop their skills and their career.

On the down side, there is considerable repetition in some amusement-park positions, which can make a job monotonous. Ride operators are frequently required to give the same long narratives during rides, and grounds department workers can find themselves repeatedly traversing the same areas to sweep up debris and empty trash containers.

Most employees who deal in any way with the public must constantly appear upbeat and exude friendliness. This can be challenging when dealing with frustrated parents and cranky children. No matter how they feel, the employees must be able to make customers feel special. This interaction must be sincerely done; guests can sense a fake facade of friendliness and be disappointed in the park's hospitality.

THE PERSONAL STORY OF AN AMUSEMENT-PARK EMPLOYEE

Ken Gleason works as a part-time cast member at Disney World, where employees are called cast members because they are "on stage" presenting a show for the guests. Ken teaches high school and finds teaching very stimulating, but he likes to be involved with people in other ways. Ken is a lifeguard at the Yacht and Beach Club Hotel. Since Ken is certified in lifesaving, he easily met the requirements for this position. However, Disney World requires its lifeguards to be specially certified through Disney, so Ken has first aid certification, CPR certification, and rescue skills certification.

Ken does not need to report to wardrobe as cast members are responsible for their swimsuits and T-shirts. After clocking in, Ken reports to the lead guard stand for his cleaning assignment. He and the other lifeguards spend two hours a day preparing the pool and the deck area for the guests. Preopening requirements are to clean and vacuum the pool, sweep and hose the deck, pick up trash, arrange the chaise lounge chairs, and wipe all tables and chairs.

At opening time, the guards meet at the lead guard stand for their daily assignments. On a typical day, each guard works three shifts of thirty minutes each at different stands and is then off stand for thirty minutes. This rotation keeps the guards fresh and alert. Ken keeps his eyes keenly focused on the activity in the water and his ears alert to sounds and whistles. While in their off period, the guards complete in-service training consisting of physical conditioning, CPR practice, and water rescue procedures.

THE FUTURE

Amusement parks have a tremendous opportunity to grow and expand their sales for a variety of reasons. Population is growing and the economy is rebounding from the doldrums of recent years. With their wide variety of exciting and entertaining attractions, amusement parks appeal to people of all ages and backgrounds. If park management can continue to offer these attractions to their guests, then patronage will continue to grow at amusement parks. This is good news for workers under the age of twenty-five who fill many of the positions in amusement parks as well as the growing number of workers in other age groups employed at these parks.

Regardless of the size or the number of rides or the type of entertainment, amusement parks represent a value to customers. Families can enter with one charge paid at the gate for almost any type of activity they may want to participate in, and they may stay for as long as they like in the day. In addition, many people no longer feel safe when at a public beach or in a public shopping area, but they do not have this concern when visiting an amusement park. While amusement parks cannot guarantee that there will never be a guest safety incident, every effort is made to provide for the safety and security of the guest. These factors contribute to the growth of amusement parks.

FOR MORE INFORMATION

All amusement parks send out information that explains their various departments and requirements for employment. One of the easiest ways to find out about employment opportunities, however, is to go online to the amusement park's website. You can find a list of amusement parks at themeparks.about.com and ultimaterollercoaster.com/resources/links/ amusement_parks. Some parks also have job hotlines. College-age students may find out more about working in parks through their university career offices because many of the large amusement parks recruit all over the country.

LOOKING AT OTHER AMUSEMENT-PARK JOBS

Around the country, there are jobs in the amusement ride industry at county and state fairs. Working in this industry may mean being a part of a traveling caravan of rides and attractions. These companies contract with fair boards to arrive and operate for specific dates. When the fair closes, the traveling amusement park packs everything and departs for the next community.

This type of business presents many unique situations for employees. First, of course, is the near-constant travel. A ride company covers hundreds of miles each week as it fulfills its obligations in one town and moves on to the next. Another unique aspect is the skill, speed, and safety requirements involved in erecting and dismantling the rides at each site. Employees work long days and nights to open a fair or to move on to the next community quickly. A third characteristic is that the rides are at county fairs where the main attractions are animal exhibits and homemaking projects. The rides are an added attraction to support this primary purpose, so the fair board will negotiate for the best price and the greatest number of operating hours.

C H A P T E R

9

CAREERS AT NATIONAL, STATE, AND LOCAL PARKS AND ORGANIZED CAMPS

A trip to a park may be no farther away than a few miles or as far away as across the country. Hundreds of millions of tourists visit national, state, and local parks each year to see animals, scenery, or historic sites. Many also return to parks year after year to enjoy the recreational aspects of these sites. Parks have such attractions as rivers, lakes, mountains, deserts, and geological formations. They also feature historical attractions, bringing history to life. Employees expand visitors' knowledge by explaining the ecology of the parks as well as any historical events that occurred there. They also maintain the quality of the park environment and ensure the safety of the visitors. Outdoor recreational opportunities are not limited to parks, of course, and many people, especially children, enjoy organized camps.

SETTINGS FOR PARKS

There are thousands of national, state, and local parks, and each of these parks employs between a few employees to several thousand.

National Park Settings

The establishment of national parks is based on the need to set aside natural, cultural, and historic areas for the enrichment of the citizens. Parks conserve natural scenery, protect wildlife and historic sites and objects, and provide for the public to enjoy these areas in such a manner as to leave them unimpaired. National parks can be divided into three categories: natural, recreational, and historical and cultural.

Natural areas include national parks that cover a large land area and preserve one or more distinctive natural land forms, wildlife habitats, or plant forms. Geysers, volcanos, caves, glaciers, waterfalls, and mountain peaks are some types of nature's creations that are protected in these parks. For example, Carlsbad Caverns in New Mexico includes massive underground chambers in a park of 48,755 acres. National monuments are not as diverse or as large as parks; they each preserve one nationally significant natural or historic resource.

Other national parks are locations where recreational activities flourish due to water and terrain. Recreational areas include recreation reservoirs, national seashores and lakeshores, national rivers, national parkways, and national trails. A unique water trail in the Everglades National Park in Florida where visitors use a kayak or canoe to enjoy the setting is an example of a recreational area.

In the historical and cultural category, parts of the history of the United States are preserved in the parks. Buildings, houses, and artifacts of a group of people as well as intangible things reflecting customs, religion, and family structure are on display. Such settings include historical parks like Appomattox Courthouse in Virginia, historical sites like Lincoln's birthplace in Kentucky, and historical memorials like Mount Rushmore in South Dakota.

National Forest Settings

About 25 percent of the land areas of the United States are classified as forest lands and are under the protection of the U.S. Forest Service. This includes 155 national forests and 20 national grasslands as well as "land utilization projects." The areas are in forty-four of the fifty states and include a total of 191 million acres of land, an area equivalent to the size of Texas. The major uses of these forests are as a water supply for people and crops; forage for grazing sheep and cattle; a home for hundreds of species of animals, fowl, fish, and insects; water recreation for the public; and timber harvesting for management of the country's resources. One national forest is Mount Hood in Oregon, with 1,058,400 acres of land featuring glaciers, lakes, springs, and alpine meadows.

State Park Settings

There are 5,655 state park areas totaling thirteen million acres. States recognize that they must protect, enhance, preserve, and wisely use natural, cultural, and recreational resources for the benefit of their citizens, and each state determines what is historically and culturally significant. Environmental interests determine land and water locations to be held by the state, so settings for state parks and forests could be acreage in forests held as nature preserves as well as settings designed to educate visitors about the geography, geology, and wildlife native to the state. Streams, rivers, and lakes are very important because boating, skiing, fishing, and swimming are leisure activities valued by the public. State parks vary enormously. Mackinac State Historic Park in Michigan showcases the island's golden past as a fort and tourist spot while Kissimmee Prairie Preserve State Park in Florida is devoted to preserving nearly seventy-five square miles of virtually unaltered landscape.

Local Park Settings

County parks and city parks are most often found in large metropolitan areas. The term *green space* is used for small tracts of land held in the public domain and used by citizens to rest, relax, and play. Municipalities may use both larger parks and green spaces to meet people's needs for a place to enjoy outdoor recreation. Swimming pools, shelters, picnic areas, walking paths, bicycle trails, and sports facilities are typically included in city parks. During the summer, programs are set up to provide activities for school-age children.

Parks in smaller communities have picnic areas and playground areas as their typical amenities, and some may have swimming pools and community centers. Although these communities generally do not have extensive daily programs, they may organize tennis tournaments and musical programs in their parks

LOOKING AT DIFFERENT CAREERS IN PARKS

Positions at national, state, and county parks vary from working as the superintendent who oversees the operation of the park to entry-level positions as part-time rangers. There are also many jobs in park services, from working in concessions to lifesaving. At city parks, employees focus on providing recreational services or maintaining the park.

Park Superintendent

State and national parks, depending on the size and the purpose of the park, may have only one manager or superintendent. More commonly, however, at national parks there is a superintendent with several assistant superintendents. The superintendent's responsibilities are to preserve natural and historical features and make these available to the public. The assistant superintendents are responsible for the departments of natural and historical features, interpretation, law enforcement and protection, park facility maintenance, and administration.

At a state park, a manager is the top authority. Depending on the size of the park, several department heads report to this person. Some examples of departments that the manager oversees are the nature center with interpretation and education, buildings and grounds maintenance, and office operations.

At a city park, the superintendent monitors the recreation programs and recreation facilities, and this could involve multiple sites. To reduce operating costs, some municipalities extend their operating capabilities by using volunteers to help the staff answer telephones and monitor leisure and education activities. While using volunteers does lower operating costs, these people must all be trained and observed, which adds to the park superintendent's responsibilities.

Park Ranger

The exact tasks that rangers have depend on the type of job held and the park where the ranger is employed. Many rangers work in the area of law enforcement, which involves ensuring that park visitors follow all laws and regulations. Duties in this area could include patrolling the waters of a lake or a ski slope. Rangers also serve as naturalists or interpreters, explaining the history or physical features of a park to visitors, creating programs, and answering questions in information centers. Rangers may also carry out various tasks associated with forest fire control; management of historical, cultural, and natural resources; and campground operation. Administrative work includes issuing visitor permits, keeping records, handling public relations, following budgets, and supervising employees. Two other areas are maintenance work, such as building trails, roads, and facilities, and conservation work to protect a park's ecosystem.

Rangers monitor use of the park's resources so that visitors do not endanger the park's ecological balance. They may need to count visitors to avoid overcrowding. In parks with camping or lodging spaces, the number of guests must not exceed space available. And rangers must check picnic areas, shelters, hiking trails, climbing areas, and water activity areas to ensure that safety problems do not occur. Other activities include monitoring fishing and hunting limits and boating safety.

In many states and national parks, rangers have rankings or levels. The position of ranger level I requires rangers to carry out a wide variety of safety and security assignments. This means knowing all park rules and the state conservation laws and interacting with visitors to maintain safe and acceptable conditions in the park. As a ranger's level increases, so does the depth of responsibilities. For example, a level III ranger functions as either the supervisor of a department in a large park or as the park manager on duty in the absence of the regular park manager at a smaller park.

Recreation Forester

Recreation foresters promote and practice good forest stewardship. Their primary responsibility is to preserve the forests for the benefit of current visitors and future visitors while keeping the integrity of the forest as a home for wildlife. A recreation forester must communicate with the public, plan and monitor recreational facilities, collaborate with biologists to protect wildlife, and work with businesses and the public in managing the forest's timber.

Park Naturalist

Naturalists conduct educational sessions for visitors on such topics as how to spot indigenous animals and plant life. They may guide tours through the park to highlight the park's natural resources. Naturalists teach in unique classrooms—from former coal mines to sand dunes to wetlands. A major part of their job is helping the public understand the fragile balance between humans and nature and between different species.

Recreation Leader

Recreation leaders are the enthusiastic and creative individuals who plan, direct, organize, and evaluate recreational programs for all of the people in a city. They must know the interests of the population and the limitations of a park in terms of space, equipment, and budget. Working with this information, recreation leaders plan individual, group, and team activities, which can include sports, games, hobbies, art, crafts, and special events.

WORKING CONDITIONS

The natural settings that encompass most parks are beautiful and peaceful and contribute to a relaxed job environment. Furthermore, the diverse range of activities, facilities, and natural attractions contributes variety to the job and stimulates creativity and problem solving. A park's management team is allowed latitude in management, decision making, and implementation of plans for the park as long as budgetary guidelines are met and the plans fit within the mission of the park's operation. As public funds exclusively support operations at many of the parks, however, the various legislators who determine the budgets for parks may reduce funding, compelling park employees to do more with less.

Maintaining a balance between visitor needs and wildlife needs is a challenge to employees at many parks. While people may wish to develop wetlands, river beds, and forests for recreational purposes, such development may endanger the environment. If parks expand to accommodate more visitors and add facilities like lodging and restaurants, the employees are criticized by environmental groups. If they don't, those wanting more public access and facilities complain. Furthermore, many parks are now overcrowded at times, which forces employees to turn people away from these popular sites. This is not well received by the public.

Closely related is the problem park employees have in managing the balance between wildlife and plant life. When the food chain is not in a state of balance, the predators of some species may be limited, contributing to an unhealthy number of another species. Deer, for example, destroy the vegetation in many parks. Without the vegetation, other species may be endangered. The decisions made by park management in these cases are always controversial.

PREPARATION FOR BECOMING A PARK EMPLOYEE

In local, state, and national parks, entry-level jobs are unskilled positions in such departments as concessions, housekeeping (when the park includes lodging facilities), grounds maintenance, and level I ranger. These positions are likely to be seasonal, depending on the weather and park usage. Previous job experience is not necessary but is helpful. A high school diploma is not required, since many of these entry-level positions are filled by high school–age people. Because parks must have reliable employees in these positions, an excellent attendance record in high school is important. Courses in communications and business are helpful for understanding how to work with people and how organizations operate. As an extracurricular activity, scouting programs teach many of the same skills that park employees need.

Most positions in parks require some skills or training. In local parks, semiskilled positions include lifeguard, recreation leader, athletic supervisor for sports programs and/or referee, clerical support, technician, and level II ranger. A level II ranger position requires the completion of two years of college with twelve or more credit hours in outdoor recreation or park management combined with six months or more of park or related work experience. To be an erosion control technician, college training is not required, but knowledge of farming practices, soils, and computer data skills are essential. To be a biology aide, laboratory science classes that teach skills in obtaining samples, completing testing, and writing reports are helpful. In place of formal educational experience, preparation for all of the semiskilled positions can be demonstrated by a work history clearly showing reliability and an ability to learn.

Highly skilled positions are held by those who work in park management. The basic educational requirement for managerial positions is a college degree. A degree in natural resources or resource management or in parks and recreation provides needed background for managing resources and facilities. People who want to work in cultural and historical parks will gain expertise from degrees in anthropology or history. Besides meeting educational requirements, candidates for highly skilled positions may need to take civil service tests to secure employment. To become a national or state park ranger, besides holding a bachelor's degree, prospective employees will typically have worked two to five years as a seasonal ranger.

As good preparation for this career, the National Park Service offers internships. To obtain an internship, it is necessary to contact a park directly. In addition, the Student Conservation Association provides high school and college students with meaningful conservation service internships and volunteer opportunities in national parks, forests, and other public lands. For information, contact:

Student Conservation Association
689 River Road
Charlestown, NH 03603-0550
thesca.org

For individuals who want to work with the United States Forest Service, degrees in forestry, wildlife sciences, or biology are good choices. A forestry major is a combination of mathematics, botanical and physical sciences, human relations, sociology, engineering, salesmanship, and business management. Biology and wildlife sciences focus more on the environment, so these degrees are good preparation for individuals who want to monitor animal habitats in forests or preserves. Business, engineering, communications, and human relations are excellent choices for a minor.

A typical urban-area park manager will benefit from a degree in parks management, recreation and leisure studies, or physical education. Counseling, business management, public relations, and communications are preferred as a minor. Secondary or elementary education degrees also provide excellent backgrounds for this position.

SPECIAL ATTRIBUTES OF PARK EMPLOYEES

Park employees spend a large part of their days working with people. Communication skills are important, and park employees must be quick thinkers. The park and its resources must be protected at all times and the visitors must be safe, so employees must be able to respond without hesitation when making a decision. Patience is necessary, too, as visitors have come from many different parts of the country or world and are curious and eager to see the entire park.

SALARY AND BENEFITS

Unskilled personnel employed in parks may earn minimum wage. Higher wages will be paid if the supply of these workers is limited. Due to the seasonal nature of many entry-level positions, benefit packages of health, dental, and life insurance may not be offered.

Salaries for rangers in national parks begin at $18,687 for a summer ranger with a college degree. Permanent ranger hires are $20,908 to $31,680, depending on education and experience. At the state level, the average starting ranger salary is $24,856. Benefits for rangers include health, dental, and medical insurance; paid vacation days; and paid sick days. Retirement plans are provided. Salary and benefits packages are controlled by the governing body. As political leaders leave office and new officials assume responsibilities, budgets for wages and salaries may be reduced, stay the same, or be increased.

City parks superintendents earn a salary based on the size of the park or park system. A city park director could earn $30,000 or more, depending on the extent of the activities and the number of park sites to be supervised. Entry-level employees at city parks receive the minimum wage or slightly higher hourly wages. Qualification for benefits depends on full-time employment. The benefits package for entry-level employees is determined by the city or county government, but typically health insurance, life insurance, paid vacation days, and retirement plans are included. The average full-time salary for recreation workers is $9 per hour.

PERKS AND PRESSURES OF BEING A PARK EMPLOYEE

Working to preserve a part of the state or country is an intrinsic part of a ranger's job, and it is also the most fulfilling part of the job. Rangers also oversee the cultural and historical preservation of our country's development, keeping the link from the past to the present strong. Knowing that they are the key to keeping living records of history is very rewarding for rangers. Educating the visitors about the environment in parks is rewarding, too. Many other park employees receive satisfaction from their contribution to maintaining and improving the environment in parks.

Park employees spend most of their time with visitors who do not know the park and its resources, so the same questions may be asked and answered repeatedly. Park employees must also know and enforce park rules. This includes verifying that the land, buildings, and water are used for the purposes intended as well as checking regularly to make certain that visitors travel where permitted on paths, trails, and roads instead of entering areas preserved for animals.

THE PERSONAL STORY OF A PARK RANGER

Before applying for a position as a ranger, Shelton Johnson worked for two summers for a concessionaire at Yellowstone National Park. Through this position, he learned about the day-to-day operations of the park.

In his first job as a seasonal park ranger at Yellowstone, Shelton was a gate ranger at the busy West Entrance Ranger Station. This job involved taking money, selling passes, issuing permits, and answering all kinds of questions. In his second year at the gate, Shelton also worked as a firefighter on the North Fork and Fan Fires that burned thousands of acres in Yellowstone. The next season, he worked in the superintendent's office in public affairs, where one of his jobs was to take the media on naturalist tours as a follow-up to the fire. When Shelton obtained permanent status, his job shifted to the chief ranger's office, where his duties were primarily clerical. However, in the winter he delivered the mail on a snowmobile on a 150-mile route.

After several other assignments, Shelton became a ranger naturalist at Yosemite National Park. His day starts with doing program development work and handling mail and correspondence. Then he works at the visitor center, answering questions from the location of the closest restroom to the name of a flower a visitor saw. He also may fix audiovisual equipment, help people find a place to stay, and in general orient people to their surroundings. Next, Shelton prepares for and then leads a ninety-minute walk. Then he returns to the visitor center for another work session. His day ends after he leads another ninety-minute nature walk.

THE FUTURE

The country's population is growing, increasing the need for outdoor spaces for fun, relaxation, and environmental education. At the same time, various species of mammals, reptiles, insects, and birds have experienced changes in their natural habitat that threaten either nature's balance or extinction of a species. Based on these two factors, the need to expand parks is great. This should result in a need for more park employees.

Funding for parks, however, has been somewhat limited in recent years due to economics. Budget cutbacks have been experienced by parks at all levels. Parks have not been closed, but the number of employees who serve the guests has been reduced. Public officials recognize the needs of the people for recreation, the country's environmental needs, and the need to preserve the history and culture of the country, so severe cuts in funding are not likely to be made. Moderate cuts in funding could occur, depending on the philosophy of elected officials and the budgeting of monies for the operation of federal, state, and local parks. Moderate cuts would mean fewer operating days, shorter hours, a reduced number of programs, and fewer employees, especially those in full-time positions.

It is important to understand that seasonal peaks and valleys of employment occur for park employees no matter how much funding is available for parks. Parks employ a small staff of full-time, year-round employees—rangers and clerical and maintenance employees. When the peak season approaches, many part-time and some full-time seasonal employees must be hired to help handle the increased volume of business. Furthermore, competition is extremely intense at all times for certain positions. Competition is also very rigorous for part-time seasonal jobs, as these jobs can lead to obtaining full-time positions. This is true at both the national and state level and in some cases at the county level.

FOR MORE INFORMATION

The following organizations have career information about becoming a ranger:

National Recreation and Park Association
22377 Belmont Ridge Road
Ashburn, VA 20148
nrpa.org

U.S. Department of the Interior
National Park Service
1849 C Street, NW
Washington, DC 20240
nps.gov

The U.S. Department of Agriculture (USDA) Forest Service has information on careers focusing on managing and improving our nation's forests and grasslands as well as on student programs:

USDA Forestry Service
1400 Independence Avenue, SW
Washington, DC 20250-0003
fs.fed.us

The Society of American Foresters' website at safnet.org has information on careers as foresters and forest technicians. It also has a job seekers' guide and a list of schools with society-recognized programs for these careers.

LOOKING AT JOBS IN ORGANIZED CAMPING

Traditionally, the term *camping* has been associated with children attending a camp for a week or more. Today, camps may use the facilities of traditional youth camps, including lodges, dining halls, and outdoor activity areas, but the campers are there for such purposes as church/fellowship, leadership, education, personal enrichment, crafts, or sport activities. Sports camps for both adults and children have become very popular in recent years and may be organized by a well-known sports star or by major universities to develop athletic skills in aspiring athletes. Adults frequently attend golf and tennis camps that last from a weekend to one or more weeks. And both adults and children attend wilderness camps that teach survival skills.

Trip camps involve using tents for shelter or carefully spaced campsites while a group of campers journey to a destination. The journey may be made by walking, biking, canoeing, sailing, horseback riding, skiing, or snowmobiling and may be for the purpose of team building, personal development, outdoor education, or exploring the outdoors.

At many camps, the only full-time employee is the on-site camp director. This individual oversees the entire operation of a camp and is often responsible for organizing and publicizing the next year's program. The director hires the staff, which includes the two key positions of director of programs and the head of housing and food. In addition, counselors, health staff, program staff, and facilities maintenance and support staff are hired.

Beside the director, a camp could also have an associate or assistant director.

All of the employees at a camp must know health and safety procedures; site, facility, and equipment maintenance procedures; and customer relations skills. Salaries for directors range from $15,000 to $50,000, depending on the size of the camp. Room and board are typically included. Due to the small size of most camp staffs, medical insurance is usually not offered.

Individuals who are interested in camp management should take college degree programs in recreation management and camp leadership. Minors in counseling, business, physical education, human relations, and hospitality management are excellent complements to this degree. Many entry-level positions are available in camps as counselors. High school students may qualify for these positions based on their skills and leadership experiences.

Leads on job opportunities can be obtained from churches, boys' and girls' clubs, 4-H extension offices, universities, scouting programs, and the YMCA. Competition for summer jobs as camp counselors is fierce. Having special qualifications like lifeguard training or first aid or CPR certification is helpful in securing a job. If an applicant is not old enough to be a counselor, he or she should consider being a counselor-in-training to get valuable job experience. The Guide to Accredited Camps has summer job information as well as professional development information. It can be obtained by contacting:

American Camping Association
5000 State Road 67 North
Martinsville, IN 46151-7902
acacamps.org

C H A P T E R

10

CAREERS AT TOURIST ATTRACTIONS

Throughout the country, there are tourist attractions that are educational as well as just plain fun to see. Some are huge, like the Smithsonian Institution in Washington, D.C., with its many exciting museums and galleries. Others are as small as roadside attractions featuring alligators and reptiles. Some tourist attractions, such as the Hearst Castle in California, may command a day or more of tourists' time. Others, like zoos and aquariums, may be easily seen in just a few hours. All of these places require employees to guide tours, sell food and souvenirs, maintain the attraction, market it, and manage the operation.

SETTINGS OF TOURIST ATTRACTIONS

Almost anything can become a tourist attraction if people show enough interest in learning more about it.

Homes and Villages

Historic homes showcase the background and lifestyle of famous citizens, including politicians, inventors, writers, political leaders, scientists, architects, actors, singers, sports heroes, wealthy industrialists, and other celebrities. Graceland Mansion, Elvis Presley's home in Memphis, Tennessee, is an example of a celebrity's home that attracts millions of visitors each year.

People are also drawn to seeing the homes of former presidents, such as Thomas Jefferson's Monticello and George Washington's Mount Vernon.

Some historic homes are good representatives of homes of a certain period in history. Natchez, Mississippi, is the oldest city along the Mississippi River, and its homes are open throughout the year to acquaint the public with plantation-era homes and the lifestyle of wealthy southern landowners.

Another setting for historical tourist attractions is an entire community. The Amana Colonies in Amana, Iowa, was one of the first communal colonies in this country, and its people lived and worked together to preserve a lifestyle of religious freedom. Their lifestyle fascinates the large number of people who visit each year to learn about the early settlers as well as how this colony functions in today's world.

Some cities represent a unique cultural aspect of present-day life and have multiple tourist attractions. One of these cities is Nashville, Tennessee, which has country and western music as its theme. Included in the attractions is the restored Ryman Theatre, where many of country music's most famous singers have performed.

Museums and Halls of Fame

Many types of museums are located throughout the country. The purpose of a museum is to preserve a unique part of the country's culture. For example, early automobiles are kept in museums to educate visitors about the development of the car as a means of transportation. Special types of cars also have museums to showcase them. The Corvette Museum in Bowling Green, Kentucky, shows the evolution of the design of this sports car.

Some museums are "living museums" that recreate the life of a period through interpreters. A replica of an 1840s village is the basis for Conner Prairie Museum in Noblesville, Indiana. As visitors walk through the homes and businesses of the village, the interpreters dress, speak, and act as though they were part of the past.

The Rock and Roll Hall of Fame in Cleveland, Ohio, gives visitors an idea about how this style of music developed and celebrates the musicians who wrote and played it. Many sports also have halls of fame, such as the Baseball Hall of Fame in Cooperstown, New York.

LOOKING AT JOBS AT TOURIST ATTRACTIONS

Even though there are a variety of tourist attractions, many of the same jobs are available at each attraction. Employees at major attractions have well-defined jobs, while those at smaller attractions will play many roles.

Guide

Almost every attraction employs guides to lead tourists through the attraction, whether it is a historic home, the Astrodome, or a wolf farm. Guides educate visitors and tell the story of the attraction's focus and exhibits. They need to be very knowledgeable about every aspect of the attraction and memorize names, dates, and facts about significant developments. Good guides couple facts with unique or unusual pieces of information; however, guides should never embellish the narrative to fascinate the visitors. Good guides must do some research to be interesting presenters.

Guides must keep their groups moving on schedule so that each group has an equal opportunity to see and hear about the attraction. They must also be observant of the actions of the visitors to ensure the safety of the visitors and the protection of the exhibits.

Security

Nearly all tourist attractions have employees involved in security, even though employees at small attractions may have other job responsibilities. One of the unique problems faced by the staff of the security department is that of keeping all parts of the exhibit in place. Visitors to tourist attractions like to take home the "real" thing from an attraction rather than purchasing a replica or a souvenir from the attraction.

Retail Sales

Sales of souvenirs, commemorative items, and food are large departments at major tourist attractions, as they play a very important role in generating income for these attractions. Managers of retail departments must have a selection of souvenirs to appeal to different age groups and different budgets.

They need full-time and part-time salespeople. Employees are also needed to manage restaurants, prepare food, serve food, and clean the facilities.

Administration

The larger a tourist attraction is, the more employees it will have working in an administrative capacity. Some attractions have large sales and marketing, accounting, computer, and human resources departments. Clerical employees are also needed, as are individuals to respond to inquiries and provide for the operating needs of the tourist attraction. Positions are available in several areas, including reservations, ticket sales, and tour programming. Large tourist attractions need professional management teams to direct all aspects of the attraction.

Maintenance and Groundskeeping

The appearance of tourist attractions is vital for capturing new visitors and repeat visitors, as well as providing for visitor safety. Due to the age of some of the structures, upkeep can be a very challenging responsibility. Some attractions have buildings listed on the U.S. Register of Historic Places, and maintenance must be done to be in compliance with this registration. Both skilled and unskilled employees are needed in the maintenance and groundskeeping department, as well as supervisory personnel.

WORKING CONDITIONS

Many major tourist attractions are open year-round, so employees have the advantage of full-time employment on a yearly basis. This contributes more readily to career development than seasonal employment would. Smaller attractions, however, may have limited hours and shorter seasons, which means many of their employees work part-time.

Nearly all tourist attractions are educational in nature. Many employees at tourist attractions take on the role of educators, teaching visitors about the past, animals, American culture, and sports, among other things. Because tourist attractions appeal to a wide audience, employees work with people of all ages, from young children to senior citizens. Most visitors have a high interest level in the attraction, since they have chosen to see it. Furthermore, many visitors are on vacation, so they are relaxed and easy to please.

There are downsides to working at tourist attractions, especially for employees dealing directly with the visitors. Typically, the attraction's features do not change, so employees must relate the same information each day. Visitors tend to ask the same types of questions, so responding to questions is repetitive. Employees must be wary of letting an element of boredom creep into the workplace. Additionally, it can be difficult to explain attractions to visitors of disparate ages and backgrounds. The presentation may go over the heads of the youngest visitors or lose the attention of the more mature visitors.

PREPARATION FOR BECOMING A TOURIST-ATTRACTION EMPLOYEE

Education requirements vary with an employee's position. Some entry-level positions, such as in guiding or retail, may be held by high school–age employees. Employers will want a mature and responsible high school student with good communication skills. Membership in student organizations as an officer or committee chairperson or participating in athletics are excellent ways to develop maturity, responsibility, and people skills. Previous work experience in hospitality or other service industries is good preparation for a career in tourist attractions. Service industry positions give excellent customer service experience.

Other positions require a high school diploma or a college degree. The amount and type of education depends on the focus of the attraction. For example, a living museum needs department heads to oversee exhibits or possibly even to conduct the tours. The depth of knowledge needed to create and develop exhibits requires a college degree. Depending on the type of museum, beneficial majors include anthropology, history, and museum studies.

Restaurants and food service at an attraction require operations management expertise. Majors that are beneficial are culinary arts, hospitality management, and business administration. For marketing and public relations positions, majors in business, communications, and media are good choices.

SALARY AND BENEFITS

Entry-level hourly positions are likely to pay minimum wage because these are nonskilled positions. In areas where the rate of unemployment is low, tourist attractions may offer higher wages to attract and keep employees in these positions. For a guide at a tourist attraction, depending on the skills needed, beginning wages may vary from slightly better than the minimum wage to $12 per hour. Positions that require some skills, such as security and maintenance, will pay more per hour. Department heads or managers earn salaries starting at $20,000 to $25,000 and may earn more depending on education and experience requirements.

Benefit packages depend on the number of employees for the attraction. Attractions that employ larger staffs are able to offer health and life insurance, retirement plans, paid vacation days, and paid sick days. Not all of these benefits are available at smaller attractions.

ADVANCEMENT

Entry-level jobs at larger tourist attractions can lead to managerial positions. For example, a tour guide could advance to senior tour guide and then to tour guide lead. From this position, advancement could continue to supervisor, assistant manager, and then manager of the guides.

THE FUTURE

Successful tourist attractions have focal points that interest their customers. Changing population demographics may affect the demand for certain types of attractions. For example, baby boomers are likely to have more leisure time and more discretionary dollars, and owners of tourist attractions will want to appeal to this large group of potential customers. Classical and historical attractions will always have business, because people want to see the lifestyles, homes, and communities of our country's pioneers. These tourist attractions are particularly interesting to school groups and senior citizens' groups. When possible, attractions should target their marketing strategies to audiences they are trying to attract.

CHAPTER 11

CAREERS IN ADVENTURE RECREATION

Rafting down the Colorado River, off-roading in the desert, bicycling through New England, and backpacking in the mountains are all trips that satisfy those who want an outdoor activity with elements of risk, physical and mental stress, and fear. Adventure recreation matches participants against elements in the environment. The goal for the participants is to overcome the challenges of the natural setting through personal skills and will. Some individuals are very interested in using their leisure time to pursue adventure recreation.

SETTINGS FOR ADVENTURE RECREATION CAREERS

The settings for adventure recreation are as diverse as the activities. These activities are associated with land, water, air, snow, or ice and include hiking, climbing, tracking, spelunking, biking, horseback riding, motorcycling, skiing, skydiving, canoeing, rafting, and scuba diving.

Survival Schools

Survival schools teach participants the skills necessary to survive in a wilderness setting for an extended period of time. They learn how to build shelters, find edible foods, and avoid dangers in the environment. Many of these schools focus on helping the participants develop self-esteem and self-reliance.

Outdoor Skills and Leadership Schools

Schools like the National Outdoor Leadership School serve people who are interested in wilderness skills, wilderness appreciation, and leadership development. These schools take people into the wilderness for an extended period, from two to twelve weeks, so they can walk out of the mountains as skilled leaders.

Whitewater Schools

Whitewater schools prepare people to be commercial whitewater guides; however, anyone who wants to become an expert in whitewater rafting may attend. Participants learn oar- and paddle-powered raft navigation, expeditioning, knot tying, river rescue and safety, equipment repair, trip logistics, guiding, menu planning, and meal preparation.

Camps for Adventure Recreation

Adventure recreation camps are found in a variety of settings and are designed for children, teenagers, and families. At Teton Valley Ranch in Kelly, Wyoming, for example, school-age boys and girls learn photography, horse packing, hiking and backpacking, swimming, ham radio operation, horseback riding, and archery while they become accustomed to being outdoors and gain readiness for handling unusual situations. The development of decision-making skills is stressed. Employees in children's adventure recreation camps must be able to work with young learners.

In recent years, adventure camps for preteen and teenage groups have become popular. Educators recognize that the camp activities can help students learn teamwork, learn about themselves, and learn to take responsibility. Teens can experience backpacking, horseback riding, technical climbing, kayaking, river rafting, fishing, glacier climbing, and wilderness survival at Wind River Wilderness Camp in Wyoming. Camp employees must present challenges appropriate to their audience.

At family guest ranches, families can be as active as they choose because the milder adventure activities, such as horseback riding, water sports, and fishing, can be done without direct supervision. Employees are responsible to have the equipment and facilities in good working order and instruct the participants in their use.

Horse packing schools have guides or outfitters teach beginning and intermediate riders in a weeklong course. Participants learn how to use equipment, tie knots, and gain expertise in horsemanship. They then set out on the trail, where they learn natural history, geology, and land ethics. Guides help direct the use of the skills learned in camp as situations occur on the trail.

Single-Activity Adventure Recreation Settings

Some adventure recreation programs concentrate on a single activity, such as mountain climbing or mountain biking. Usually, participants pick an activity because they have had some experience with it, but sometimes a novice chooses one for the adventure experience. Skill level and ability are critical for these activities. It is up to the outfitter or the guide to determine that all participants are capable, because others may be at risk if one individual is not capable.

Some settings are just mildly adventurous, such as a self-guided houseboat excursion on a lake. However, even then participants must have basic instruction on how to use the equipment. There is no risk-free situation or activity. All employees must educate participants on safety and other procedures relevant to the adventure recreation.

Narrow-Audience Adventure Recreation Settings

Adventure recreation activities can focus on a particular audience. One example is the Red Mountain Spa in Utah, which caters to fitness enthusiasts who also want the pampering, luxury, and relaxation of a full-service spa. Guides lead activities that help participants improve their overall level of fitness.

Specific-Interest Adventure Recreation Settings

Some adventure attractions appeal to participants with a specific interest. People interested in water and sea life might spend a week seeing whales, sea lions, porpoises, bird life, and natural beaches while sea kayaking in Mexico's Bay of Whales. Guides on this adventure must have the ability to supervise people moving at different paces. They must also educate the participants on what they are seeing as well as closely monitor weather conditions to keep all participants safe.

Another example of a specific-interest recreation activity is a mountain-climbing trek in the Grand Tetons in Jackson Hole, Wyoming. Leaders train the participants in rope handling, climbing signals, climbing harnesses, methods of anchoring, and placing protection, then judge their readiness and capabilities. Throughout the climb, the leaders make certain that everyone is using correct techniques.

LOOKING AT A CAREER AS A GUIDE

The major responsibility of guides is to oversee the safe undertaking of an adventure. Included in this are the tasks of educating and training the participants, checking equipment, keeping track of weather conditions, leading the group, organizing meals and overnight stays, and keeping the group informed of pertinent information regarding the weather and terrain. The safety aspect of the adventure is of primary importance. During the trip, the guide must be aware of the actions of the participants at all times. In a group activity, one individual's careless action can endanger everyone, so all participants must practice safety. Guides can also be described as trip leaders, chefs, safety experts, musicians, storytellers, environmentalists, and teachers.

WORKING CONDITIONS

Depending upon the activity, the adventure recreation season may last for several months or year-round. Seasonal employment is very common because so many activities are dependent upon the weather. Employees must then find other employment for the remainder of the year.

Guides are expected to work long days, typically from twelve to fourteen hours. Guides, as well as outfitters for adventure recreation companies, primarily work outdoors. Their work environment includes swirling waters, lofty mountain peaks, and native forests. In small companies, the owner and head guide are the same person. Seasonal guides are hired to help with the excursions. Larger adventure companies have a year-round staff of ten to more than one hundred employees to carry out the marketing, planning, purchasing of supplies, accounting, and human resources functions. In small companies, the owner handles most of these responsibilities.

Adventure recreation activities can be risky. Guides must always focus on the safety of the participants. They may have to change routes or postpone an activity if the weather or other event causes unsafe conditions. Making decisions affecting the participants' safety can be stressful for guides.

PREPARATION FOR BECOMING A GUIDE

Part-time or seasonal jobs in support areas help prospective guides learn about an activity. Developing a personal interest in a particular recreation activity and following it as an avocation is another helpful step in becoming a guide. Survival schools can give a future guide solid knowledge of the precautions and commonsense applications necessary for potentially dangerous adventure activities. Many adventure recreation companies have their own schools or require guides to have attended a wilderness instruction school. When hired, guides typically work with other guides until they are ready to go out on their own, which could take as long as a year for very challenging activities.

While in high school, students can begin to prepare for careers in adventure recreation by getting CPR certification and first-aid training. Courses in the life sciences, the physical sciences, history, and communication should be useful in any kind of adventure activity. Extracurricular activities, such as joining a ski club, climbing club, or walking club, provide experience in outdoor activities and equipment use and maintenance. Leadership activities are helpful in learning to work with and direct the activities of other people, as an understanding of group dynamics is essential to knowing how to get group cooperation. The principles learned in scouting are valuable in any type of outdoor job. College degrees that may be helpful are geography, geology, forestry, wildlife, and anthropology.

Specific skills must be learned by adventure recreation guides, and most whitewater outfitters require their guides to have school training. Whitewater schools prepare people for the different degrees of difficulty of rapids and teach them how to use equipment and employ safety measures. Swift water rescue training is also taught, along with CPR and first aid.

SPECIAL ATTRIBUTES OF GUIDES

Guides must be excellent decision makers. Good judgment and common sense are important characteristics to support a guide's ability to make sound decisions. Maturity and a calm manner are key personality traits, as participants may react with concern in situations where the danger risk becomes uncomfortable. Guides assess the degree of danger; if conditions are such that injury could occur, they make alternatives plans and activities. If the degree of risk is appropriate for the skill level of the group, the guide will direct them to proceed. The calmness of the guide will convince the participants of the correctness of this decision.

Guides must be in good physical condition. Their work hours are very long, and they must perform very strenuous activities. Physical conditioning to maintain their stamina and strength is essential.

SALARY, BENEFITS, AND ADVANCEMENT

What beginning guides earn depends on the region where they work, the skills required, and the size of the company where they work. Beginning guides can earn between $50 and $70 per day. They can increase their earnings by taking on additional responsibilities, such as driving participants to and from recreation sites. Top experienced guides earn $150 or more a day. Some guides are paid by the trips they take.

Guides who work for very small companies or work part-time usually do not receive benefits. Larger adventure companies with many full-time employees offer life and health insurance. Salaries for these individuals could be in the range of $20,000 to $40,000. Company owners/operators have the greatest opportunity to make larger salaries. A guide can advance to a trip leader position and then to a management position in a larger company.

THE PERSONAL STORY OF A GUIDE

As a guide on horseback adventure trips, experienced rider Jerry Porter's day begins early in the morning when he checks the travel conditions for the day. Then he directs the setting-up, service, and cleanup of breakfast. After the morning meal, Jerry confirms that all of the participants are ready and that equipment checks are completed. If camp is being broken, he oversees all of the packing for transportation.

Before embarking on the day's activity, Jerry reviews safety procedures. Leading the group through the activity requires him to use the technical skills required by the activity. During the ride, he watches out for emotions or fright on the part of the participants; watches for signs of fatigue; and looks out for carelessness or clowning around, which might cause an accident. During the day, Jerry discusses interesting facts about the area and its plants and animals and answers questions. He controls the pace of the group's activity, allowing for rest breaks, snacks, and meals.

At the end of the day, Jerry oversees the setting-up of the camp and the preparation of the evening meal. Equipment checks are made and any necessary repairs are initiated. The next day's activities are previewed and the weather is checked for any changes in the forecast.

THE FUTURE

Adventure recreation companies have a good potential for growth. More people are learning about these vacation activities and groups are beginning to use the activities of adventure companies for a wide variety of purposes. Businesses see adventure recreation as a team-building exercise; group dynamics come into play and business associates learn to appreciate the value of being a team member. Some judicial courts use adventure recreation as a way to help orient troubled juveniles in the right direction. These youths can learn how to take responsibility for their actions, build self-confidence, and accept directions from the guide through adventure recreation.

FOR MORE INFORMATION

Individuals who are interested in adventure recreation can obtain information from:

National Outdoor Leadership School
284 Lander Street
Lander, WY 82520-2848
nols.edu

Outward Bound USA
100 Mystery Point Road
Garrison, NY 10524
outwardbound.org

12

CAREERS IN MEETING PLANNING

The International Reading Association holds one huge annual meeting as well as regional and state meetings. Most large corporations, such as Bank America and General Motors, have annual meetings. Some companies and industry groups have executive get-togethers at resorts. Professional and social organizations use meetings as a major form of communication within their groups. All of these meetings have to be planned down to the last detail. While meeting planning is not a new concept, it has become a formal career.

LOOKING AT A CAREER AS A MEETING PLANNER

The meeting planner has the overall responsibility for the quality of a meeting. Attendees' time at a meeting is wasted unless they can concentrate, function properly, and leave with new insights or information. Failing to plan a meeting properly can result in lost business in the future for independent meeting planners.

A meeting planner must follow many steps to ensure a quality meeting. The planner initiates all plans for a meeting, including setting objectives; creating themes appropriate to the meeting's purpose; designing the agenda; and estimating time for all activities, including breaks, refreshments, and movement between areas. Selecting the meeting site is a planner's responsibility. Organizational tasks include coordinating with needed support groups such as the staff of a hotel, restaurant, or caterer; arranging transportation; planning the menu; selecting speakers; marketing literature on the meeting to obtain the maximum number of attendees, if necessary; and arranging the exhibits. The planner must also determine how much a meeting will cost or stay within a previously agreed-upon budget. The final step is for the meeting planner to evaluate the meeting using as criteria every aspect of the meeting—time, location, cost, food, lodging, quality of speakers, and entertainment.

WORKING CONDITIONS

Meeting planners may have their own businesses where they contract with associations and companies to plan meetings as needed, or they may work within large corporations or associations to plan all of the events that are held by that enterprise. In many instances, meeting planners have control and flexibility over their work hours. Independent meeting planners can choose to plan as many meetings as they can competently handle.

Most of the time meeting planners work from their office. They also may work in different locations because meetings are held at different sites within a city or in different cities around the country or the world.

Meeting planners who are independent operators must continuously submit proposals to obtain business. Hard work goes into preparation for a proposal, and the planner may or may not be selected. This gives an element of uncertainty to the life of the planner.

During the actual days of a meeting that has been planned, planners are on site or on call twenty-four hours a day. They must be available to resolve any problems that arise. Plus, they need to do a considerable amount of standing, lifting, walking, and kneeling when directing the setup for an event. The pressure of keeping track of hundreds of details before and at events can be mentally tiring. These long days at meetings may make it difficult to handle other clients, as well as to spend time with families and friends.

PREPARATION FOR BECOMING A MEETING PLANNER

A meeting planner is not required to have a degree; however, professional organizations for the industry, like Meeting Professionals International, highly recommend postsecondary training. A solid choice of a college major for this career is a hospitality management program focusing on operations management or, if offered, courses in meeting and convention management. These courses help future planners learn the principles and procedures of meeting planning. Other majors that would be appropriate are business administration, marketing, communications, and public relations. Any of these areas could also serve as a minor. Coursework in media and computer applications would support the activities of a meeting.

Whether or not an individual completes a degree, professional certification is recommended. Meeting Professionals International has training and an examination to become a certified meeting professional.

Many meeting planners begin their careers as assistants to professionals in the field. Related work experiences in the hospitality industry in hotels or with catering companies can be beneficial. These experiences provide an excellent opportunity to work with groups and get a general feel for some of their activities.

Volunteer experiences can also enhance a career in meeting planning. Organizing a prom, a fund-raiser, a blood drive, or a marathon teaches organizational and event-coordination skills.

SPECIAL ATTRIBUTES OF MEETING PLANNERS

Attention to detail is one characteristic that all meeting planners must have. Every aspect of a meeting needs to be considered and planned for. A meeting planner must also be cool, calm, and collected. Even carefully constructed plans are not always followed by other individuals. Mistakes happen, and accidents occur; the meeting planner must create feasible alternatives. The most important thing is to not panic. Other characteristics of meeting planners include solid communication skills, the ability to identify problems, and people management skills.

SALARY AND BENEFITS

Meeting convention planners' incomes vary, with hourly wages ranging from $15 to more than $25. Their average annual income is more than

$43,000. Independent planners make the most at more than $60,000 per year, followed by corporate planners, association planners, government planners, university planners, and religious-organization planners. Independent planners must carefully negotiate compensation with the person or organization requesting his or her services to be sure it is fair to both parties. Independent planners also generally need to provide their own insurance and retirement plans. If a planner is a part of a large organization, the company's benefits package typically includes health and life insurance, paid vacation days, paid sick days, and retirement plans.

ADVANCEMENT

Large firms have three levels of staff, and it may be possible to move from one level to another. The facilitator handles basic tasks, such as choosing menus and working with a hotel. The technician may be responsible for running reservations and registration, finding and setting up a site, and operating the budget. The professional designs and sells the events, creates the budget, and oversees all operations. Some meeting planners advance by moving to larger companies or by setting up their own companies.

THE FUTURE

The future looks very promising for meeting planners. Corporations have found meetings to be an effective and efficient way to educate employees on new developments or to update skills. Associations meet for monthly, quarterly, or annual meetings to conduct their business. Groups of businesses, such as car, boat, and electronics manufacturers, display their new products at huge convention centers. All these meetings require planners. Furthermore, hotels, resorts, conference centers, convention centers, and exhibition halls can accommodate the smallest and largest groups of people. With the demand for meetings and the locations to hold those meetings, meeting planners should be busy bringing these two elements together. Nevertheless, the employment outlook for meeting planners is highly dependent upon the economy. Economic downturns result in fewer meetings as businesses and associations reduce their spending.

FOR MORE INFORMATION

Meeting Professionals International has a journal, publications, and online learning courses. More can be learned about this organization by writing 1950 Stemmons Freeway, Suite 5018, Dallas, Texas 75207-3109, or visiting their website at mpiweb.org. Other associations to contact are

Convention Industry Council
8201 Greensboro Drive, Suite 300
McLean, VA 22102
conventionindustry.org

Exposition Services and Contractors Association
2260 Corporate Circle, Suite 400
Henderson, NV 89074-7701
esca.org

Hospitality Sales and Marketing Association International
8201 Greensboro Drive, Suite 300
McLean, VA 22102
hsmai.org

International Association of Conference Centers
243 North Lindbergh Boulevard
Saint Louis, MO 63141
iaccglobal.org

International Association of Conference and Visitor's Bureaus
2025 M Street NW, Suite 500
Washington, DC 20036
iacvb.org

LOOKING AT OTHER MEETING-PLANNING JOBS

Special event planning is closely tied to meeting planning. Events include shows, expositions, celebrations, dances, and competitions and are commonly one-time affairs. These events rarely focus on business matters. The event may be open to an entire community rather than only participants who are aligned with a particular organization or business.

Individuals who organize special events plan in the same detail-oriented fashion as meeting planners. Special event planners must secure a location that is the right size and location. They also handle such things as securing advertising, finding food vendors, meeting city licensing requirements, removing trash, monitoring safety and parking, and coordinating temporary staffing needs for the event. For the duration of the event, the planners are there on site to oversee the execution of all of the planning. One example of a special event is the Gus Macker basketball tournament, which moves from location to location around the country. Its directors hire a special event company at each site to take care of all local arrangements.

C H A P T E R

13

CAREERS AT HOTELS, MOTELS, AND OTHER LODGINGS

Hotels, motels, and other accommodations vary just as much as the families and business travelers who stay in them. The lodging industry offers places to stay from upscale hotels to bed-and-breakfast inns.

SETTINGS FOR LODGINGS

Lodging accommodations began as stopover, resting places for travelers en route to a destination. Today, many resort hotels and inns have become the destination itself. Pools, nightclubs, fine restaurants, and convention centers are some of their attractions. The lodging industry has emerged throughout the world as one of the largest generators of jobs. There are more than sixty-one thousand establishments offering lodging in the United States, providing a wide variety of overnight accommodations to suit different needs and budgets from senior citizens to corporate travelers to families. Hotels and motels today fall into the following categories:

• **Commercial.** Cater mainly to businesspeople, tourists, and others needing accommodations for just a few days. Larger hotels and motels have banquet rooms, exhibit halls, and spacious ballrooms to accommodate conventions, business meetings, wedding receptions and other social events.
• **Resort.** Offer a variety of recreational facilities, such as swimming pools, golf courses, tennis courts, and health spas as well as planned social

activities and entertainment. They are usually located in vacation destinations near the seashore, mountains, and other attractions. Some have convention and conference facilities.

• **Residential.** Have living quarters for permanent and semipermanent residents. They combine apartment living with the convenience of hotel services. Many have dining rooms.

• **Extended stay.** Combine the features of a resort and a residential hotel. Guests usually stay for a minimum of five consecutive nights. Rooms typically have fully equipped kitchens and office spaces with computer hookups, and guests have access to fitness centers.

• **Casino.** Have lodging in hotel facilities and a casino on the premises. Some also have conference or convention facilities.

Besides hotels and motels, lodging is also available at bed-and-breakfast inns, campgrounds, and boarding houses for overnight guests.

LOOKING AT LODGING JOBS BY DEPARTMENT

The key ingredient for the success of the lodging is the personnel, and it's a given that larger lodgings have more employees. Some large facilities have as many as a thousand employees. Each hotel or motel will have its own organization, and job responsibilities will vary from lodging to lodging. There is, however, a similarity in the way lodging facilities are organized. And the larger the facility, the more specialized the jobs will be. The two simple organizational charts in Figures 13.1 and 13.2 show how a small and a large lodging could be organized. Figure 13.1 shows the organization of a small lodging facility of 100 to 150 rooms that does not have food or beverage service. Figure 13.2 depicts the organization of a large facility with a great number of departments.

In the lodging industry, employees are usually described as having jobs in "the front of the house" or "the back of the house." Employees who work

Figure 13.1 Organization chart for a small lodging facility.

Figure 13.2 Organization chart for a large lodging facility.

Source: American Hotel and Lodging Association

directly with the guests have jobs in front-of-the-house departments, which include front office, marketing and sales, food and beverage, security, human resources, uniformed service, and accounting and financial management. The back-of-the-house departments are housekeeping and facility maintenance. Although employees in back-of-the-house departments may not have much direct contact with guests, their work is vital to guest approval of a lodging facility.

Front Office

The front office is often regarded as the "nerve center" of the hotel. The front office is where the guests check in and out, make payments on their accounts, and retrieve messages. The front desk staff should be people oriented, good at solving problems, and attentive to details. Positions at the front office include rooms division manager, front desk clerk, reservationist, front office manager, mail and information clerk, and switchboard operator.

Housekeeping

A lodging property's main product is the guest room. The housekeeping personnel are responsible for keeping the rooms ready for guests. They take pride in maintaining property cleanliness and are constantly monitoring guests' comfort and safety. Positions in housekeeping include executive housekeeper, inspector, floor supervisor, houseperson, room attendant, laundry personnel, and linen-room worker.

Marketing and Sales

Without guests, no hotel can survive. It is the job of the marketing and sales personnel to discover what guests want, decide how to build guests' needs into the services sold, and know how best to reach potential guests.

The creative efforts of this team can bring in the business that makes a property a success. Positions in marketing and sales include the marketing director, sales manager, public relations, account executive, advertising representative, banquet sales manager, and convention services representative.

Food and Beverage

Food and beverage sales can mean big business. The quality of the food being served and the quality of service are the keys to a successful department. Positions in the food and beverage department include the food and beverage director, host/captain/maitre d'hotel, chef/cook, wine steward, dietitian, food server, banquet services worker, steward/dishwasher, baker, cashier/checker, restaurant manager, dining room manager, kitchen manager, and shift leader.

Security

The members of this department must master the fine art of balancing guest relations with safety and security. The security staff is charged with protecting the safety and security of guests, fellow employees, and the property. They also develop and direct all emergency procedures. Positions on the security staff include the director of security and house officer.

Human Resources

Human resources is responsible for recruiting, selecting, and training qualified applicants. It also administers benefits programs and handles other personnel matters. Positions in human resources include the benefits administrator, employment manager, human resources director, and training manager.

Facility Maintenance and Engineering

The engineering and maintenance staff members are responsible for property equipment and systems. Fixing and maintaining electrical systems, plumbing, heating, ventilation, air-conditioning, and refrigeration are highly skilled and highly respected jobs in the hospitality industry. Positions in the facility maintenance and engineering field include engineer, grounds maintenance worker, plumber, painter, electrician, and carpenter.

Uniformed Service

The members of the uniformed service staff greet guests, assist with travel plans, and much more. These employees are always on the go and play a vital role in making guests feel welcome. Positions in this department include the bell captain, concierge, parking attendant, door attendant, and courtesy van operator.

Accounting and Financial Management

Accounting and finance personnel use their professional foresight to help guide management decisions, make important financial recommendations, and even forecast industry trends to help the hotel succeed. This department records sales, controls expenditures, calculates costs, and keeps close track of overall profits. Positions in accounting and financial management include controller, accountant, bookkeeper, purchasing agent, cashier, auditor/night auditor, clerk, credit manager, and computer systems worker.

LOOKING AT A JOB AS A FRONT DESK CLERK

More than 160,000 hotel and motel desk clerks work in front office departments. They perform a variety of services for guests in lodging establishments and play a major role in establishing a hotel's reputation for service and courtesy. They consider the guests' preferences in assigning rooms while trying to maximize the lodging's revenues. They answer questions about services, checkout times, and the local community. They inform housekeepers, telephone operators, and maintenance workers which rooms are occupied. They collect payment for rooms and issue receipts. In addition, they may take reservations for future stays at the facility. In smaller hotels and motels, desk clerks may also act as bookkeeper, advance reservations agent, cashier, and/or telephone switchboard operator.

WORKING CONDITIONS

A front desk clerk's job offers very flexible work schedules. A full-time front desk clerk can work any of three different eight-hour shifts. More than one in five clerks works part-time, and some clerks in resort areas may be seasonal employees. Lodging facilities are located throughout the world, making these jobs available in most locations. There is a very high turnover rate associated with this job. Opportunities for part-time work should continue to be plentiful because the front desk must be staffed twenty-four hours a day.

PREPARATION FOR BECOMING A FRONT DESK CLERK

Most lodging facilities prefer applicants with at least a high school education and experience in the field for this position. Most high schools offer courses in bookkeeping and computer skills that give applicants the clerical skills they will need on the job. Future desk clerks can gain important work experience by having a part-time job or summer employment in an office or a retail store or an entry-level position in a lodging facility. It is even better for applicants to have specialized training with hospitality-specific courses in a technical school or a community college. Furthermore, the Educational Institute of the American Hotel and Lodging Association offers training through the Internet, videos, textbooks, study guides, and seminars. Many desk clerks are trained on the job by an experienced front desk clerk or manager.

SPECIAL ATTRIBUTES OF FRONT DESK CLERKS

Because such an important part of front desk clerks' jobs is dealing with people, this position requires individuals to have a friendly, outgoing personality and a desire to serve people. They also need to be well groomed, polite, dependable, and sincere. A good memory for faces and names as well as an understanding of human nature are also good qualities. Most clerks need computer skills, and clerical, mathematical, and bookkeeping skills are also helpful.

ADVANCEMENT

Clerks who have more experience and a better education in the field are more often considered for advancement to managerial positions. Most large lodging facilities offering managerial training programs begin their trainees in front desk clerk positions to have them gain experience in hotel services. Trainees then begin to advance up the career ladder to such positions as reservations manager or front office manager.

SALARY AND BENEFITS

Front desk clerks' income depends on factors such as geographical location and size of the lodging facility, the type of employing organization, and the experience and training of the individual worker. For example, clerks at large luxury hotels generally are paid more than clerks at budget establishments. Beginning clerks earn between minimum wage and $9 per hour. Clerks with three years of experience with the same employer can earn close to $12 per hour. Overall, the average hourly earnings are more than $8 per hour. In some lodging facilities, front desk clerks may also receive paid vacations, reduced lodging rates, free meals, and medical insurance.

THE PERSONAL STORY OF A FRONT DESK CLERK

Seth Fulk began his career in hospitality as an assistant manager at a pizza restaurant while he was in high school. He chose to work in hospitality because he was intrigued by people. As a freshman studying hospitality management, his school required him to work five hundred hours in the hotel/restaurant field to receive his degree. The school helped Seth get his job as front desk clerk at an all-suites hotel in a major metropolitan area. He worked an eight-hour day five days a week while still attending school.

Seth's responsibilities included checking guests in and out, fulfilling guest requests, taking reservations, and assisting all management personnel. He also handled a variety of other services for the hotel. On the night shift, especially, he could find himself helping other departments—for instance, making beds for housekeeping late in the evening.

Seth received his training on the job, primarily from coworkers but also from the manager. According to Seth, the necessary skills for this job are people skills, problem-solving skills, and basic computer skills.

LOOKING AT A CAREER AS A MANAGER

For vacationing families and out-of-town businesspeople, a comfortable room, good food, and a helpful hotel staff can make being away from home an enjoyable experience. Managers and assistant managers ensure that each guest's stay is a pleasant one. Managers are responsible for the efficient and profitable operation of the hotel or motel. The duties of a manager depend on the size, type, and location of the lodging facility. In smaller lodging facilities, a single manager may be in charge of all aspects of the operations. In large facilities, managers may be aided by a number of assistant managers who head different departments.

General Manager

The general manager has the overall responsibility for the operation of the hotel. The owners and executives of the hotel chain establish guidelines. Within those guidelines, the general manager sets room rates, allocates funds to the different departments, approves expenditures, and sets the standards for guest service, decor, housekeeping, food quality and service, and banquet operations.

Assistant Managers

Assistant managers must make sure that the day-to-day operations of their departments meet the manager's standards. They assign department workers to shifts, give out work assignments, schedule staff vacations, and promote workers within the departments. This position is generally filled by employees already working at a facility.

Resident Managers

Resident managers live in hotels and are on call twenty-four hours a day to resolve any problems or emergencies, although they normally work an eight-hour day. As the most senior assistant manager, a resident manager oversees the day-to-day operations of the hotel. In many hotels, the general manager also serves as the resident manager.

WORKING CONDITIONS

Since lodging facilities are open twenty-four hours a day, 365 days a year, working nights and weekends is not uncommon for hotel and motel managers. Most lodging facilities' managers work more than forty hours per week. Managers sometimes have to coordinate a wide range of functions. Conventions and large groups of tourists may present unusual problems. Dealing with irate patrons and difficult employees can be stressful.

PREPARATION FOR BECOMING A MANAGER

Reaching the managerial level is based upon training, experience, and individual initiative. In the past, most managers were promoted from the ranks of front desk clerks, housekeepers, waitstaff and chefs, and hotel sales workers. Today, postsecondary training in hotel or restaurant management is preferred for most hotel management positions, although a college liberal arts degree may be sufficient when coupled with related hotel experience. Any experience working in a hotel is an asset to all persons seeking hotel management careers.

A bachelor's degree in hotel and restaurant administration provides a strong starting point for a career in lodging management. These programs usually include instruction in hotel administration, accounting, economics, marketing, housekeeping, food service management and catering, hotel maintenance engineering, and data processing. (See Appendix D for a list of schools offering hospitality degree programs.) Some colleges even have campus lodging facilities where students can work. Individuals who cannot afford to attend college can take courses from the Educational Institute of the American Hotel and Lodging Association.

Sometimes large hotels sponsor specialized on-the-job training programs that let trainees rotate among various departments to gain a thorough knowledge of the hotel's operation. After demonstrating their knowledge and administrative ability in lodging operations, trainees may advance to department heads and on to assistant managers and managers. Some hotels may help finance the necessary training in hotel management for outstanding employees.

SPECIAL ATTRIBUTES OF MANAGERS

Lodging managers need to have people skills that equip them to get along with all kinds of people, even in stressful situations. They also need to have initiative, self-discipline, and the ability to organize and direct the work of others.

ADVANCEMENT

Most hotels promote employees who have proven their ability. Large hotel and motel chains may offer better opportunities for advancement than small establishments, but relocation every several years is often necessary for advancement in these chains. Career advancement can be accelerated by completion of certification programs offered by industry associations.

SALARY AND BENEFITS

What managers and assistant managers earn varies greatly according to their job responsibilities and the size of the hotel in which they work. Facilities with less than one hundred rooms pay managers an hourly range from $7.00 to $14.50. Those with one hundred or more rooms pay between $9.00

and $22.00 an hour or more. A few managers earn $10,000 or more a month.

In some hotels, managers may earn bonuses of up to 20 percent of their basic salary. In addition, they and their families may be furnished with lodging, meals, parking, laundry, and other services. Most managers and assistants receive three to eleven paid holidays a year, paid vacation, sick leave, life insurance, medical benefits, and pension plans. Some hotels offer profit-sharing plans, educational assistance, and other benefits.

THE PERSONAL STORY OF A GENERAL MANAGER

Michael Conner decided on a career in the lodging industry after a family trip that included stays in hotels. The day after he graduated from high school, he took a job as a busser at a hotel in Indianapolis. At the same time, he took classes in the hotel and restaurant management program at a vocational college. The hotel management knew of Michael's interest and gave him experience by cross-training him. Michael worked in catering and reservations and also had jobs as a desk clerk, telephone operator, bellperson, and reservationist.

After Michael received his associate's degree, he stayed on at the school and started working as a culinary assistant. In this job, Michael assisted the chef, did purchasing for the school's culinary classes, and arranged catering functions with the chef. During this time, he also worked, when needed, at the hotel in the catering department. After working for a year at the school, he heard about a new hotel opening and secured a job there as a desk clerk. At the same time, he vowed to get into the hotel chain's management training program. Within six months, he was in the program, which was a great hands-on learning experience. Soon he was involved in the opening of a new hotel. Then he was promoted to front desk manager, which meant he was an assistant manager taking care of front desk administrative tasks, including overseeing reservations, administering staff payroll, and the hiring and disciplining of employees. After a company restructuring, he became assistant general manager of the hotel, running the housekeeping, maintenance, restaurant, and sales and marketing departments.

When Michael was in college, he set the long-term goal of being a general manager by the time he was thirty. He achieved this goal when he was only twenty-five years old and was assigned the task of opening a new property for the hotel chain. He saw the hotel being built from the ground up and had the responsibility of selecting the entire staff of twenty-three people. Michael was charged with the responsibility of having the hotel ready to open four weeks after it was built; he exceeded all expectations and had it ready in two weeks.

After two years as a general manager, Michael was recruited by another hotel chain to return to his home state as general manager of an economy property that did not have a restaurant. Michael was the only manager at this lodging facility and had the responsibility of running the housekeeping, front office, and maintenance departments.

THE PERSONAL STORY OF A SALES MANAGER

Convention hotels with many rooms and loads of space for meetings have salespeople to bring conventions to these hotels. This is exactly what Brian Sabones is doing as a major market sales manager at the largest convention hotel in Chicago.

Brian spent nine months training in the hotel chain's corporate management program—five months rotating through the many departments of the hotel and four months in the sales department learning about hotel sales and being a sales manager. His first job was as a small meetings sales manager, booking meetings for groups that would need one hundred sleeping rooms or fewer. About 50 percent of the business came to him, and he had to go and find the rest.

After eighteen months, Brian was promoted to major market sales manager, booking up to seventeen hundred sleeping rooms as well as the convention space each group needed. Most of the groups that he booked were associations, as they hold the most meetings. Because his territory is Washington, D.C., Brian travels to that city one week out of every two months to visit clients and let them know how important they are to his hotel.

Brian enjoys his job because it allows him to interact with so many people. He also likes the opportunity that this job gives him for future promotions. The next steps would be to become an associate director of sales managing small meetings managers, and then the director of sales overseeing the entire sales department.

THE PERSONAL STORY OF A FOOD AND BEVERAGE DIRECTOR

Suresh Rao is executive assistant manager of food and beverages in a large, full-service, upscale hotel. After studying economics in college, he decided on a career in the hospitality industry because he wanted to work in different hotels and see the world. His first position was as a busser in a large intercontinental hotel chain in India. Suresh then moved to Europe where he received extensive on-the-job training and learned to speak several languages, including Dutch, Flemish, and German. He came to the United States to work as an assistant manager at a hotel that was part of a large international chain. He was soon promoted to food and beverage director at another hotel in the chain. Then he worked for several other chains.

Today, Suresh is in charge of the overall operation of the hotel's food and beverage department, which includes all food and beverage outlets in the hotel, catering, and room service. This includes overseeing the purchasing of food; ensuring the quality of the food; handling the hiring and scheduling of employees; and working for revenue growth and profitability in his department. Suresh supervises 150 people, and the executive chef, the restaurant manager, the director of catering, the banquet manager, and the executive steward report directly to him. These individuals supervise the staff members within their departments.

Suresh generally works six days a week and enjoys his job because it is challenging and no two days are alike. He likes seeing satisfied guests and employees enjoying their jobs. His special joy is helping people advance within the industry and achieve their career goals.

THE PERSONAL STORY OF AN EXECUTIVE HOUSEKEEPER

Archie Henderson was a police officer when he began working part-time in the security department of a full-service, upscale hotel. The head housekeeper noticed that Archie was always cleaning up after people and offered him a job in housekeeping. Archie started out as a management trainee called a team leader who was responsible for the cleaning of a section of the hotel. Archie had to supervise employees who had limited education and little career enthusiasm, but Archie soon discovered that he had a knack for dealing with people, and within eight months, his section was the cleanest in the hotel. Archie did no cleaning; he just supervised and trained the workers and participated in the hiring of new employees. Archie also handled paperwork and inspected each room for cleanliness and other details.

Archie was soon promoted to assistant executive housekeeper. His responsibilities included checking on other team leaders, the public space workers, and the overall cleanliness of the hotel. He also managed the payroll and ordered all supplies while staying within the budget.

The harder Archie worked, the more promotions he received. Soon he was the executive housekeeper, just two years after beginning as a management trainee. Within three months, Archie went to a bigger hotel in the chain to serve as one of two assistant executive housekeepers. Within one year, Archie was the executive housekeeper at this facility, with two assistants and eleven team leaders.

Archie left the hotel field to go into business for himself for a while. But soon he found himself back in housekeeping at a luxury hotel. After another career interruption to help family members with health problems, he worked briefly for another hotel as an executive housekeeper before moving to his present job.

For the past three years, Archie has been an executive housekeeper at a full-service, upscale hotel, handling a staff of 116 employees. When he was hired, this hotel was close to failing the chain's quality standards for cleanliness. Within four months, he had won the general manager's traveling trophy award for the most improved department; turning the housekeeping department around involved spending a lot of time training the employees. While working hard on the job, Archie has also been taking classes to increase his expertise in management. He has earned a Human Resources Management Certificate and is working on getting housekeeper certification from the American Hotel & Lodging Association.

THE FUTURE

Both the number of people employed in hotel and lodging and their salaries are expected to grow faster than the average for all occupations through the year 2012. This is because more lodging facilities will be built and business travel and domestic and foreign tourism will continue to grow as the economy is improving. Employment outlook in this industry varies by job.

Because a growing share of the industry is composed of economy properties, the number of manager jobs is expected to grow slowly because economy properties generally have fewer managers than full-service hotels. Typically, economy hotels have a general manager, and regional offices of the hotel management company employ department managers, such as executive housekeepers, to oversee several hotels. Even though industry growth will be concentrated in the economy sector, full-service hotels will continue to offer many training and managerial opportunities.

Employment for desk clerks is expected to grow rapidly as they assume responsibilities that were previously reserved for managers. Employment of other clerical workers will grow more slowly because of the spread of computer technology. Job opportunities will be good in cleaning, especially in larger accommodations. Employment in food service will grow slowly, reflecting the number of establishments that do not have full-service restaurants.

FOR MORE INFORMATION

Individuals can learn more about the lodging industry by visiting the website of the American Hotel and Lodging Association at ahla.com. The organization has a career center with information on schools, scholarships, and high school programs at its Educational Institute website at ei-ahla.org or by calling 800-344-4381 or 517-372-8800.

Vocational schools, community colleges, and universities in the United States and abroad offer courses in hospitality management. For a fee, the International Council on Hotel, Restaurant and Institutional Education (CHRIE) has a CD-ROM guide to accredited programs in hospitality and tourism that lists schools with hospitality programs as well as career advice.

CHRIE
2613 North Parham Road, Second Floor
Richmond, VA 23294
chrie.org

CHAPTER
14

CAREER OPPORTUNITIES IN RESTAURANTS

The restaurant industry is the second largest employer in the United States—only the government employs more people. According to the National Restaurant Association, nine hundred thousand locations serve more than seventy billion meals and snacks every year. Because the restaurant business is so labor intensive, more than twelve million people, or approximately 9 percent of the country's workforce, work in this industry. The opportunities for employment continue to grow as more and more people choose to eat out more often each year.

There are two main kinds of restaurants: sit-down restaurants and fast-food restaurants. In 1994, sales in fast-food restaurants surpassed those in sit-down establishments for the first time. The history of fast-food restaurants is quite short; McDonald's was established in 1948 and Wendy's in 1969.

LOOKING AT JOBS IN RESTAURANTS

Just like the lodging industry, restaurants have front-of-the-house and back-of-the-house employees. Typically, those working in the front have contact with customers. Sit-down restaurants may employ the following positions:

bar managers

bussers

cashiers

dining room managers

dining room supervisors

head waitstaff

hosting staff

server assistants

sommeliers

waitstaff

wine stewards

Individuals who are involved with the preparation of food are the back-of-the-house employees. Within this group at sit-down restaurants are:

chefs

cooks

dishwashers

executive chefs

kitchen managers

kitchen supervisors

kitchen workers

pastry chefs

prep cooks

sous-chefs

At fast-food restaurants, front-of-the-store employees take orders, take money, and assemble or pack orders. Back-of-the-store employees cook and prepare food and clean the equipment.

LOOKING AT JOBS IN SIT-DOWN RESTAURANTS

Whether in small, informal diners or large, elegant restaurants, all food-service workers deal with customers. The quality of service they provide determines in part whether the patron is likely to return. The efficient and profitable operation of restaurants depends on the skill of their managers and assistant managers.

LOOKING AT A CAREER AS A RESTAURANT MANAGER

Although restaurant cuisine, prices, and settings vary greatly, restaurant managers have many responsibilities in common. To run an operation both efficiently and profitably, managers and assistant managers must select and appropriately price interesting menu items, order and effectively use food and other supplies, achieve consistent quality in food preparation and service, recruit and train an adequate number of workers and supervise their work, and attend to the various administrative aspects of the business.

In most restaurants, the manager is assisted by one or more assistant managers, depending on the size and business hours of the establishment. In large or fine-dining establishments, the management team consists of a general manager, one or more assistant managers, and an executive chef. The executive chef is responsible for the operation of the kitchen, while the assistant managers oversee service in the dining room and other areas of the restaurant. Much of the administrative work—payroll, paying suppliers, and record keeping—is handled by bookkeepers. In restaurants that operate long hours, seven days a week, the manager is aided by several assistant managers, each of whom supervises a shift.

WORKING CONDITIONS

Managers are often the first to arrive and the last to leave and frequently work fifty or more hours a week. They also work evenings and weekends, since these are popular dining periods. Being a manager can be very high-pressure, especially during peak dining hours, when the manager must simultaneously coordinate a wide range of activities, handle problems with irate customers, and deal with uncooperative employees.

PREPARATION FOR BECOMING A RESTAURANT MANAGER

Prospective restaurant managers need a combination of experience, education, and training.

Requirements

Many restaurant manager positions are filled by promoting experienced food-service employees. Waitstaff and chefs who have demonstrated their potential for handling increased responsibility sometimes advance to assistant manager or management trainee when openings occur. General managers need experience working as assistant managers.

Most restaurant chains prefer to hire managers with degrees in food-service management, although they hire graduates with degrees in other areas who have demonstrated interest and aptitude. A list of postsecondary schools offering programs or degrees in restaurant management is given in Appendix D. Some programs combine classroom and laboratory study with internships that provide on-the-job experience. Many online courses are also available through such organizations as the National Restaurant Educational Foundation at nraef.org.

Restaurant management can be demanding, so good health and stamina are important. Self-discipline, initiative, and leadership ability are absolutely essential. Managers must be able to solve problems and concentrate on details. They need good communication skills to deal with customers, employees, and suppliers, as well as a neat and clean appearance.

Training and Certification

Restaurant chains have rigorous formal training programs for individuals hired for management jobs. Through a combination of classroom and on-the-job training, trainees receive instruction and gain work experience in all aspects of the operation of a restaurant, including food preparation, nutrition, sanitation, security, company policies and procedures, personnel management, record keeping, and the preparation of reports.

Recognition of professional competence is shown by restaurant managers who have earned the designation of Foodservice Management Professional (FMP). The Educational Foundation of the National Restaurant Association awards the FMP to managers who have earned food protection manager certification and spent a minimum of two or three years of supervisory experience in a restaurant or food-service operation.

SALARY, BENEFITS, AND ADVANCEMENT

Earnings of restaurant managers vary greatly, depending on their responsibilities and the type and size of the establishment. Overall, their average annual earnings are close to $36,000. The lowest-paid 10 percent of this group have a base salary of slightly more than $21,000, while the highest-paid 10 percent earn close to $68,000. Most receive bonuses based on their performance. In addition to receiving typical benefits, most salaried managers receive free meals and the opportunity for additional training, depending on their length of service.

Assistant managers can become managers. Managers typically advance by relocating to larger restaurants or regional management positions within chains. Some managers open their own restaurants, while others advance to hotel management positions in food service.

THE PERSONAL STORY OF A RESTAURANT MANAGER

Jay Chandler began his restaurant career working at a pizza restaurant when he was in high school. When he graduated from college with a degree in business management, he started his restaurant career as the general manager of a small, full-service Mexican restaurant. He then transferred to a steak house in a site that had been converted from an old railroad station. Jay stayed at this job for one and a half years, often working as many as ninety-five hours a week. His next job was as assistant manager of a smorgasbord restaurant. Then this company gave him the task of opening a new restaurant and serving as general manager. After a short stint in sales, he returned to the restaurant world to work in a cafeteria chain.

Jay worked at eleven different locations of the restaurant chain and advanced up the career ladder from service manager to general manager. As general manager, he oversaw the entire operation of a restaurant with the help of three assistant managers: the chef, who made up the menus and ordered inventory for the kitchen; the service manager, who made sure that the servers and housekeeping staff were doing their jobs correctly; and the line supervisor, who made sure that the food line looked neat and tidy. To become a manager, Jay had to complete a twenty-three–week training program that covered everything from cleaning to knowing the four hundred different recipes that the cafeteria offered.

During Jay's tenure at this location, the cafeteria had four record sales years and four record profit years. He appreciated that the company said employees would work only five days a week and meant it. He also liked working for a stable company that cared about family values.

THE FUTURE FOR RESTAURANT MANAGERS

To meet the ever-increasing demand for consuming meals outside the home, more restaurants will be built and more managers will be needed to supervise them. Future managers can expect to find more jobs working for national chains, as fewer new restaurants are independently owned and operated. Job opportunities will be best for those who have a bachelor's or associate's degree in restaurant or food-service management. This occupation is growing about as fast as the average for all occupations.

PREPARATION FOR OWNING A RESTAURANT

Many restaurant owners have come up through the ranks from entry-level positions, while others have been restaurant managers. Anyone thinking about opening a restaurant must realize that there is no guarantee of success. Competition among restaurants is intense, and many restaurants do not survive. Here are some of the steps that are involved in opening a restaurant:

- Gain restaurant experience before opening a restaurant.
- Develop a business plan that includes price range of the food, staffing and inventory requirements, hours of operation, and projected sales and earnings.
- Create a market study that includes the expected clientele, type of restaurant, and atmosphere of restaurant.
- Hire a lawyer.
- Select a site.
- Research codes, ordinances, and permits.
- Secure adequate financing.
- Consider franchise opportunities.
- Organize the restaurant: select the menu, plan the layout, and choose the staff.

THE PERSONAL STORY OF TWO RESTAURANT OWNERS

Mary and Kammel Emeish decided to open a restaurant featuring Middle Eastern food because they believed that there was a demand for this type of food and they were familiar with this cuisine. They chose a location in an area that had high restaurant traffic. After making sure they had adequate financing, they leased a building for their restaurant. Then they designed the layout of the restaurant, with the help of an architect to maximize the use of the available space, and bought equipment. Before opening, they had to secure a number of permits and licenses, especially liquor licenses, and to make sure that the restaurant met health board inspection requirements. They also had to establish bank procedures so that they could accept credit cards. Then they advertised their restaurant's grand opening and advertised for help. They wanted a small staff of dependable people who could be counted on to help with everything. The Emeishes themselves planned to work at the restaurant, with Mary doing most of the cooking.

Mary and Kammel enjoyed the restaurant that they established. They liked the successes and challenges it brought them and the compliments of their customers. They did not like the twenty-four-hour-a-day nature of running a restaurant nor putting their personal lives on hold. They also discovered that they could not count completely on their staff. They advise future restaurant owners to make sure that they have the money, desire, and time to commit to a business that will play such a big role in the owners' lives.

LOOKING AT THE JOBS OF CHEFS, COOKS, AND OTHER KITCHEN EMPLOYEES

Every restaurant needs a reputation for serving good food, whether hamburgers and french fries or exotic foreign cuisine. The reputation of a restaurant depends greatly on its back-of-the-house employees—chefs, cooks, and other kitchen employees—as they determine the quality of the food that is served.

The type of food a restaurant serves establishes the personnel who are needed to prepare it. A restaurant with menu items that are time consuming and difficult to prepare may need a staff with several chefs and cooks, sometimes called assistant or apprentice chefs, and many less-skilled workers. In these kitchens, each chef or cook usually has a special assignment and often a special job title—vegetable, fry, or sauce cook, for example. Casual dining restaurants often feature a limited number of easy-to-prepare items, supplemented by short-order specialties and ready-made desserts. Typically, one cook prepares all of the food with the help of a short-order cook and one or two other kitchen workers. A restaurant with a menu of sandwiches and hamburgers needs only a fast-food or short-order cook with limited cooking skills.

RESPONSIBILITIES BY DEPARTMENT

There are varying levels of responsibility in the kitchen staff.

Executive Chefs

Executive chefs coordinate the work of the kitchen staff and often direct certain kinds of food preparation. They decide the size of servings, plan menus, and buy food supplies.

Chefs and Cooks

Chefs and cooks prepare meals that are tasty and attractively presented. Chefs are the most highly skilled, trained, and experienced kitchen workers. Although the terms *chef* and *cook* are sometimes used interchangeably, a cook generally has more limited skills. Many chefs have earned fame for both themselves and the restaurants where they work because of their skill in preparing traditional favorites, creating new dishes, and improving familiar ones.

Restaurant chefs and cooks generally prepare a wide selection of dishes for each meal, cooking most individual servings to order. They are often responsible for directing the work of other kitchen workers, estimating food requirements, and ordering food and kitchen supplies. Some chefs and cooks also help plan meals and develop menus.

Bread and Pastry Bakers

Bread and pastry bakers—called pastry chefs in some kitchens—produce baked goods for restaurants. They bake breads, rolls, pastries, pies, and cakes, doing most of the work by hand.

Short-Order Cooks

Short-order cooks prepare foods to order in restaurants and coffee shops that emphasize fast service, often working on several orders at the same time. Prior to busy periods, they may prepare food for cooking. During slow periods, they may clean the grill, the food-preparation surfaces, the counters, and the floors.

Other Kitchen Employees

Other kitchen employees perform tasks requiring less skill; they work under the direction of chefs and cooks. They weigh and measure ingredients, fetch pots and pans, and stir and strain soups and sauces. They clean, peel, and slice vegetables and fruits and make salads. They also may cut and grind meats, poultry, and seafood in preparation for cooking. Their responsibilities also include cleaning the work areas, equipment, dishes, and silverware.

WORKING CONDITIONS

Working conditions depend to some degree on the age of the kitchen. Many restaurant kitchens have modern equipment, convenient work areas, and air-conditioning, but others are not nearly as well equipped. Workers generally must work close together. And there are job hazards from working near hot ovens and grills and lifting heavy pots and pans. Kitchen employees may slip, fall, and cut or burn themselves; however, relatively few serious injuries occur.

Restaurant work frequently includes weekend, holiday, and evening hours because these are the times that customers wish to eat out. Half of all short-order and fast-food cooks and other kitchen workers work part-time. A third of all bakers and restaurant cooks work part-time. Vacation resorts may offer only seasonal employment.

PREPARATION FOR BECOMING A CHEF, COOK, OR KITCHEN EMPLOYEE

Individuals can start working in the less-skilled jobs in restaurant kitchens with no experience. With on-the-job training, they can learn to be assistant or short-order cooks. To become a chef or a cook in a fine restaurant, many years of training or schooling are necessary. While a high school diploma is not required for beginning jobs, it is recommended for those planning a career as a cook or chef.

An increasing number of chefs and cooks are getting their training through high school or postsecondary school vocational programs and two- or four-year college programs. Training in these schools is primarily hands-on, and the subjects are much the same in every school. Students learn to prepare food and to use and care for kitchen equipment. Course topics often include planning menus, sizing portions and controlling food costs, purchasing food supplies in quantity, selecting and storing food, and using leftover food to minimize waste. Students also learn hotel and restaurant sanitation and public health rules for handling food. Training in supervisory and management skills is sometimes emphasized in courses offered by private vocational schools. There are also a variety of correspondence and Internet courses. Apprenticeship programs, typically lasting three years, are offered by professional culinary institutes, industry associations, and trade unions. In addition, some large hotels and restaurants operate their own training programs for cooks and chefs. The armed forces are also a good source of training for jobs as chefs and cooks.

SPECIAL ATTRIBUTES OF CHEFS, COOKS, OR KITCHEN EMPLOYEES

To be a successful chef, cook, or kitchen employee, it is absolutely essential to have an interest in food. Chefs and cooks must also be creative in concocting new recipes and must stay current with food trends. The ability to work as part of a team, a keen sense of taste and smell, and personal cleanliness are important attributes that chefs, cooks, and other kitchen workers should possess. Furthermore, it is important to have good health; most states require health certificates indicating that restaurant workers are free from contagious diseases.

ADVANCEMENT

The restaurant industry is one place where the American dream is possible—individuals can start in entry-level positions and end up being chefs or even restaurant owners. However, individuals who have courses in commercial food preparation may be able to start as a cook or chef as well as have an advantage when looking for jobs in better restaurants. An additional asset in climbing the career ladder is to have certification, which is based on experience and formal training. The American Culinary Federation certifies various levels of chefs, pastry professionals, and culinary educators.

Advancement opportunities for chefs and cooks are numerous. Many acquire higher-paying positions and new cooking skills by moving from one job to another. Besides culinary skills, advancement also depends on ability to supervise lesser-skilled workers and limit food costs by minimizing waste and accurately anticipating the amount of perishable supplies needed. Some cooks and chefs gradually advance to the executive chef level while others advance into supervisory or management positions; some will eventually go into business as caterers or restaurant owners, while still others become instructors in vocational programs in academic institutions.

SALARY AND BENEFITS

The salaries that chefs, cooks, and other kitchen workers earn depend greatly on where they live and where they work. The more elegant and fine a restaurant is, the higher the salary at all levels. Executive chefs may earn more than $65,000 a year. "Superstar" chefs can earn more than $200,000 a year. A few chefs increase their income by writing cookbooks and appearing on television. The median hourly earnings for chefs and head cooks is about $13.50 per hour, restaurant cooks receive about $9.00 per hour, and cafeteria cooks earn slightly less. Short-order cooks and food preparation workers earn close to $8.00 per hour.

Some employers provide uniforms and free meals. However, federal law permits employers to deduct from wages the cost of any meals or lodging provided, and some employers exercise this right. Benefits such as paid vacation, sick leave, and health insurance are available for full-time restaurant employees. Part-time workers usually do not receive these benefits.

In some large hotels and restaurants, kitchen workers belong to unions. The principal unions are the Hotel Employees and Restaurant Employees International Union and the Service Employees International Union.

THE PERSONAL STORY OF A CHEF

Dieter Puska was born in Austria. His family was in the retail and food business, so he has been around food all his life. He trained to be a chef and served as an apprentice for three years. Through working at different hotels and restaurants, Dieter gained more experience and also had the opportunity to travel. He chose a job in Cincinnati, but on his arrival in the United States, he was transferred to Indianapolis to be a sous-chef and has remained there ever since.

In 1976, Dieter decided to open his own restaurant, the Glass Chimney, which has been widely acclaimed for its excellence. The restaurant offers fine dining in a sophisticated setting. Dieter created the menu and was the chef.

In 1980, Dieter opened another restaurant next door to the Glass Chimney and called it Deeter's. This restaurant had a more casual atmosphere than his first restaurant. As in his first restaurant, only the best-quality food was creatively prepared and served. Subsequently, Dieter joined with a friend to start an even more casual restaurant called Deeter's & Gabe's—a rotisserie with an open kitchen.

Dieter's day begins at Deeter's & Gabe's, where he writes the specials of the day and checks to make sure everything is running smoothly. He then goes to his office at the Glass Chimney and does paperwork. He also runs errands to places like the post office and the bank. In the afternoon, he checks on the operation of the Glass Chimney and Deeters. As the executive chef, he no longer cooks all the time, only stepping in when needed. In the evenings, he usually spends some time at both the Glass Chimney and Deeter's, supervising the operation and greeting patrons. On his way home, he stops by Deeter's & Gabe's, finally arriving home about midnight.

Dieter offers these suggestions to people wanting to have a career like his: take classes, work in good establishments, and try to get a lot of hands-on experience. Dieter enjoys his career because he can be creative and try different ideas. He also likes that customers become friends after a while. The negative to his career is that it is hard on family life. Even on holidays, he has to make sure that everything is running smoothly and the customers are satisfied.

THE FUTURE FOR CHEFS, COOKS, AND KITCHEN EMPLOYEES

Job openings for chefs, cooks, and other kitchen workers are expected to be plentiful in the near future; however, competition for jobs in the top kitchens of high-end restaurants will be keen. The overwhelming majority of job openings will come from the need to replace workers who leave this occupation. Higher-skilled chefs and cooks will find more jobs in casual rather than upscale restaurants because of the increasing draw of informal dining. Employment of fast-food and short-order cooks will be slower than for others in this occupation.

LOOKING AT JOBS IN FAST-FOOD RESTAURANTS

Fast-food restaurants employ 3.5 million workers. Everyone is familiar with the speedy workers at these outlets who handle so many jobs at once. There are two basic job categories. The front-of-the-store workers take orders and serve customers, and the back-of-store workers work solely on food preparation.

A job at a fast-food restaurant is often the first formal job that a teenager holds. Most workers are young people between the ages of sixteen and twenty who begin as hourly workers. Many of these young workers are in high school; however, some are college students trying to earn money for school expenses. And recently, more and more workers in these restaurants are homemakers who want to work part-time or retirees who enjoy working or welcome the income.

LOOKING AT A JOB AS AN HOURLY EMPLOYEE

Whether fast-food employees are employed at Burger King, Wendy's, or another fast-food restaurant, their duties are quite similar. Typically, hourly workers do a variety of tasks during each shift. Surprisingly, they also have some managerial responsibilities, especially training and supervising other employees. The job tasks performed by hourly workers include:

assemble or pack orders

bus or clear tables

clean equipment

clean parking lot

clean restrooms

cook food

fill out payroll, paperwork,
 inventory

hire workers

host in dining room

order food and supplies

prepare food (noncooking)

relieve manager

sell by suggestion

supervise workers

sweep or mop floors

take money

take orders

train workers

unload trucks

PREPARATION FOR BECOMING AN HOURLY EMPLOYEE

Fast-food workers are trained in a variety of ways. Some workers receive formal training, in which each step in the training process is spelled out in a manual. Other workers receive casual, on-the-job training. They are shown what to do, and then attempt to do it themselves. Restaurants that are owned by well-known chains or a franchise with a large number of units usually give new workers well-organized, standardized training. Besides considerable hands-on experience, training also may consist of reading materials, listening to tapes, and watching slide shows, videos, or films.

ADVANCEMENT

The fast-food industry is unusual in that it offers entry-level workers a realistic opportunity to become managers if they demonstrate the requisite abilities. A large number of today's fast-food company executives are former hourly employees who worked their way up. A chairman of the board of McDonald's was once a grill man. And no one in the White Castle organization—except for certain specialized jobs—can be in management without having started at the bottom of the ladder as a crew worker.

Within most large chains, the first step up from hourly crew worker is to crew trainer. Crew trainers normally perform the same jobs as crew workers with the added responsibility of training new hourly workers. The next step is shift leader, where their major responsibility is to manage the people on a shift. Shift leaders also may assume responsibility for the restaurant when the assistant manager or manager is not on duty. Promising shift leaders also spend time learning the assistant manager's duties. It could take from six months to one year for a crew member to become a trainer, and six months to two years or more to become a shift leader.

SALARY AND BENEFITS

At one time, hourly employees were hired at the minimum wage, and that was where they stayed. But labor shortages in some areas, plus the need for more skilled workers, have made starting wages for fast-food workers more competitive with other entry-level jobs. Hourly employees also can expect regular wage increases, perhaps as many as three in the first year for effective employees. As entry-level workers advance up each level from being a crew team member, they will usually increase their hourly pay by a dollar.

In the past, standard benefits programs for full-time hourly employees did not begin until they had been employed for six months to a year. In areas with labor shortages, full-time workers are now eligible for benefits earlier, and some companies are enrolling part-time workers, too. Packages are becoming more generous and include paid sick leave and paid vacations along with health and life insurance and retirement plans. In addition, they may get free or half-price meals while they are on duty. Uniforms are free and may even be laundered by the company.

THE PERSONAL STORY OF AN HOURLY EMPLOYEE

Linda worked at a fast-food restaurant for two summers and during her senior year in high school. She was usually a front-of-the-store worker, although at times she worked in the back. At either task, she did some cleaning. When the manager did not have enough workers on a shift, Linda would have to cover both the front and back of the store.

When Linda worked at the front of the store, she operated the cash register and took orders. She or a helper would make drink orders for the customers. During peak hours, she would also assemble orders. At the end of her shift, she would clean the dining room as well as stock spoons, napkins, cups, and dessert dishes for the next shift.

As a back-of-the-store worker, Linda cooked food on the grill. She would also clean the back area, which included the floors, the large walk-in refrigerator, and the bathrooms, as well as take out garbage and put new linings in the garbage pails. No matter where she was working, Linda would be assigned at times to wash windows, sweep outside, and clean the video games.

LOOKING AT A CAREER AS A FAST-FOOD RESTAURANT MANAGER

Typically, a fast-food restaurant has a manager, sometimes called a general manager, and one or more assistant managers, who may have different titles. Managers and assistant managers have a tremendous number of responsibilities in seeing that a restaurant runs smoothly every day. Their responsibilities include employee supervision and training, restaurant operations, and administration. They may assign seventy or more workers to staff different positions in a restaurant that is open up to twenty-one hours a day—or even a restaurant that never closes. Furthermore, they may also keep track of money that adds up to more than a million dollars a year in sales in a single restaurant. Few jobs offer a young person such a responsible position.

WORKING CONDITIONS

Work is fast-paced and demanding at fast-food restaurants. It is necessary to work shifts, some of which begin early in the day, while others extend into the wee hours of the morning. Hours can be long, particularly for assistant managers and managers. Ten-hour days are common, as are fifty-hour weeks. In addition, weekend and holiday work is required at times.

PREPARATION FOR BECOMING A FAST-FOOD RESTAURANT MANAGER

Individuals can start in an entry-level position and climb the management ladder as they gain experience. Or they can attend a two- or four-year college and then begin as assistant managers. Most fast-food chains have formal training programs for assistant managers and managers. Assistant managers usually begin training in the restaurant, where they are taught what is done at each crew station and how to manage a shift. Once the basics are mastered, trainees work side-by-side with the manager or a training manager to learn the necessary skills. A company manual specifies exactly what must be learned and gives trainees additional information about the job. The next step almost always is attending five days of formal classes at a regional training center. Then the trainees return to the restaurant to polish their skills. Trainees may also take additional one- or two-day courses at the training center. Assistant managers in restaurants that do not have training centers learn on the job and by reading company manuals.

Most future managers begin with in-store training by the managers, who gradually teach them the jobs that a manager performs. The managers also help them select the company classes and seminars they should take. Depending on the chain, managers often attend a one- to two-week management course at a management training center, either before they become managers or sometime in their first year in that position. Graduates of management courses are usually eligible to take further courses on a single management skill.

ADVANCEMENT

The manager is at the top of the ladder in the restaurant but can keep climbing. A talented individual may even reach the very top—president of a large chain or a large franchise. One step up the ladder is the district manager, who is almost always promoted from within the company and who generally oversees the operation of three to seven stores. An area manager—the first level of upper management—generally supervises five to ten district managers. A regional vice president plans, organizes, and controls the operations and growth of the region. The senior vice president of operations is in charge of the operation and growth of the restaurants, and the president is responsible for all aspects of the company.

SALARY AND BENEFITS

Managers' salaries can be good. But they become even better for assistant managers, managers, and district managers who meet performance and sales goals when they are paid bonuses based on store profits. Some fast-food managers with as little as five years of experience are making more than $50,000 a year. There is the possibility of participating in the profit-sharing plans of your employer, in which companies share a certain percentage of the profits with their employees. Managers also receive standard benefits packages.

THE PERSONAL STORY OF A FAST-FOOD RESTAURANT MANAGER

Keith Crane rapidly ascended from a starting team member at a major fast-food chain to manager/co-owner of a pizza franchise. He began at the bottom rung but immediately showed management that he was willing to work hard as well as to substitute for employees who called in sick. Soon, he worked at other close-by restaurants in the chain when they were short-handed. His dependability quickly led to his becoming a crew chief and then a shift manager. He then trained to become an assistant manager by working with the manager and showing her and the director of operations that he could apply the techniques learned in the training manual to store operations. Before Keith could become an assistant manager, however, he and several other managers in the chain joined together to open a newly franchised pizza restaurant.

THE FUTURE OF THE FAST-FOOD INDUSTRY

Fast food is the giant of the restaurant industry. As long as busy Americans eat so many meals in restaurants, the future of fast food is secure. Furthermore, the trend of offering some healthy items, such as lettuce-wrapped sandwiches, attracts more customers. Employment opportunities for entry-level workers are excellent now and are likely to remain so in the near future. The number of fast-food units will grow, creating new jobs, and there is considerable turnover in the fast-food labor force. In many areas of this country, there are shortages of workers to fill both entry-level and managerial positions.

Another appealing aspect of working in this industry is the rapid advancement of management personnel. Many executives in high-level positions are only in their thirties and forties.

FOR MORE INFORMATION

The Educational Foundation of the National Restaurant Association offers tools and tips for building a successful career in the restaurant industry. The association has both scholarship and internship programs. It also offers information on certification as a Foodservice Management Professional. Contact:

The Educational Foundation of the National Restaurant Association
175 West Jackson Boulevard, Suite 1500
Chicago, IL 60604-2814
nraef.org

For information on courses that meet the standards of the American Culinary Federation Association, visit the organization's website at acfchefs.org. Appendix D has a list of schools that provide restaurant and food-service programs.

APPENDIX

A

TRAVEL SCHOOLS

On-the-job experience with a travel agency was once the usual source of training for travel agents. Now most agencies require more formal training. The American Society of Travel Agents provides this list of member travel schools.

UNITED STATES

Arizona
Maricopa Skill Center
Phoenix, AZ
msc.gwc.maricopa.edu

California
Academy Pacific Travel College
Hollywood, CA
academypacific.com

Foothill College Travel Careers
Los Altos, CA
bss.foothill.fhda.edu/tc

International Tour Management
    Institute, Inc.
San Francisco, CA
itmitourtraining.com

Los Medanos Community College
    Travel Program
Pittsburg, CA
losmedanos.edu

Connecticut
Odyssey Expedition Institute
Brookfield, CT
odysseyexpeditions.org

Florida

Cruise Agent Only–Cruise
   University
Fort Lauderdale, FL
cruiseagentonly.com

Florida International University
North Miami, FL
fiu.edu

Mid Florida Tech
Orlando, FL
mft.ocps.net

Illinois

Career Quest Training Center,
   Inc.
New Lenox, IL
careerquesttraining.com

College of DuPage
Glen Ellyn, IL
cod.edu

Moraine Valley Community
   College
Palos Hills, IL
morainevalley.edu

Northwestern Business College
Chicago, IL
northwesternbc.edu

Waubonsee Community College
Sugar Grove, IL
waubonsee.edu

Indiana

Physical Education and Tourism
   Management
Indianapolis, IN
iupui.edu/~indyhper

Kansas

Bryan Travel College
Topeka, KS
bryancareercolleges.com

Massachusetts

Northern Essex Community
   College
Haverhill, MA
necc.mass.edu

Maine

Andover College
Portland, ME
andovercollege.com

Michigan

Lansing Community College
Lansing, MI
lansing.cc.mi.us

Minnesota

Dakota County Technical College
   Travel & Tourism Program
Rosemount, MN
dctc.mnscu.edu

Missouri

Saint Louis Community College
Saint Louis, MO
stlcc.cc.mo.us

North Carolina

Central Piedmont Community
   College
Charlotte, NC
cpcc.cc.nc.us

Travel Agent Training Center, Inc.
Matthews, NC
travelagenttrainingcenter.com

New Hampshire

New Hampshire Technical
   Institute
Concord, NH
nhti.edu

Nevada

Community College of Southern
   Nevada
North Las Vegas, NV
ccsn.nevada.edu

New York

Genesee Community College
Batavia, NY
sunygenesee.cc.ny.us

LaGuardia Community College
Long Island City, NY
lagcc.cuny.edu

Monroe Community College
Rochester, NY
monroecc.edu

National Academy Foundation
New York, NY
naf.org

Niagara University
Niagara University, NY
niagara.edu

State University of New York
   at Delhi
Delhi, NY
delhi.edu

Ohio

Bradford School
Columbus, OH
bradfordschoolcolumbus.edu

Columbus State Community
   College/Hospitality
   Management
Columbus, OH
cscc.edu

Sinclair Community College
Dayton, OH
sinclair.edu

Oregon

Mount Hood Community College
Gresham, OR
mhcc.edu

Pennsylvania

Bradford School
Pittsburgh, PA
bradfordpittsburgh.edu

Central Pennsylvania College
Summerdale, PA
centralpenn.edu

Education Direct
Scranton, PA
educationdirect.com

Luzerne County Community
  College
Nanticoke, PA
luzerne.edu

Reading Area Community College
Reading, PA
racc.edu

York Technical Institute
York, PA
yti.edu

Rhode Island
Community College of
  Rhode Island
Warwick, RI
ccri.edu

Johnson & Wales University
Providence, RI
jwu.edu

Texas
El Paso Community College–
  Rio Grande Campus
El Paso, TX
epcc.edu

Utah
Education Systems/Travel Campus
Sandy, UT
travelcampus.com

Salt Lake Community College
Salt Lake City, UT
slcc.edu

Virginia
Northern Virginia Community
  College
Annandale, VA
nv.cc.va.us

Omega Travel School
Fairfax, VA
owt.net/school

Washington
Edmonds Community
  College/Travel and Tourism
  Department
Lynnwood, WA
edcc.edu

Wisconsin
Milwaukee Area Technical College
Oak Creek, WI
milwaukee.tec.wi.us

CANADA

Ontario
Algonquin College
Ottawa, ON
algonquincollege.com

A P P E N D I X

SCHEDULED AIRLINES

The airline employment picture changes constantly. Applicants should visit airlines' websites or contact their human resources departments for up-to-date information, job requirements, and training program availability. The following list of scheduled airlines is provided by the Air Transport Association of America. You can access a list of regional carriers at the website of the Regional Airline Association at raa.org.

Alaska Airlines, Inc.
P.O. Box 68900
Seattle-Tacoma International
   Airport
Seattle, WA 98168-0900
alaskaair.com

Aloha Airlines
P.O. Box 30028
Honolulu, HI 96820-0228
alohaairlines.com

America West Airlines, Inc.
4000 East Sky Harbor Boulevard
Phoenix, AZ 85034
americawest.com

American Airlines
P.O. Box 619616
Dallas–Fort Worth Airport, TX
   75261-9616
aa.com

ASTAR Air Cargo, Inc.
Two South Biscayne Boulevard,
   Suite 3663
Miami, FL 33131
astaraircargo.us

ATA Airlines
P.O. Box 51609
Indianapolis International Airport
Indianapolis, IN 46251-0609
ata.com

Continental Airlines
1600 Smith Street
Houston, TX 77002
continental.com

Delta Airlines
P.O. Box 2070
Atlanta, GA 30320
delta.com

DHL Airways
P.O. Box 75122
Cincinnati, OH 45275
dhl.com

Evergreen International Airlines
3850 Three Mile Lane
McMinnville, OR 97128-9496
evergreenaviation.com

Federal Express Corporation
942 South Shady Grove Road
Memphis, TN 38120
fedex.com

Hawaiian Airlines
P.O. Box 30008
Honolulu International Airport
Honolulu, HI 96820-0008
hawaiianair.com

Jet Blue Airways Corporation
118-29 Queens Boulevard
Forest Hills, NY 11375
jetblue.com

Midwest Airlines, Inc.
6744 South Howell Avenue
Oak Creek, WI 53154
midwestairlines.com

Northwest Airlines
Minneapolis–St. Paul
    International Airport
St. Paul, MN 55111-3075
nwa.com

Southwest Airlines
Box 36611 Love Field
Dallas, TX 75235-1625
southwest.com

United Airlines
P.O. Box 66100
Chicago, IL 60666-0100
united.com

UPS Airlines
1400 North Hurstbourne Parkway
Louisville, KY 40223
ups.com

USAirways, Inc.
2345 Crystal Drive
Arlington, VA 22227
usair.com

SCHOOLS OFFERING TOURISM COURSES

The following schools offer travel and tourism courses leading to certificates, associate degrees, and bachelor degrees. The list of schools is provided by the National Tourism Foundation.

UNITED STATES

Alabama

Auburn University
Auburn, AL
auburn.edu

Faulkner State Community
    College
Bay Minette, AL
faulkner.cc.al.us

Mobile Technical Institute
Mobile, AL
alboenha.state.al.us

Tuskegee University/College of
    Business
Tuskegee, AL
tuskegee.edu

University of Alabama
Tuscaloosa, AL
ches.ua.edu

University of South Alabama
Mobile, AL
southalabama.edu

Worldwide Travel Institute
Northport, AL
worldwidetravelinstitute.com

Alaska

Alaska Pacific University
Anchorage, AK
alaskapacific.edu

Career Academy
Anchorage, AK
careeracademy.net

University of Alaska
Fairbanks, AK
uaf.edu

Arizona
Arizona State University
Tempe, AZ
asu.edu

Central Arizona College
Coolidge, AZ
centralaz.edu

East Valley Institute of
Technology
Gilbert, AZ
evtpc.org

Northern Arizona University
Flagstaff, AZ
hrm.nau.edu

Pima Community College–East
Campus
Tucson, AZ
tourismeducation.com

Arkansas
Arkansas Tech University
Russellville, AR
atu.edu

Garland County Community
College
Hot Springs, AR
gccc.edu

Henderson State University
Arkadelphia, AR
hsu.edu

Phillips Community College
Helena, AR
pccua.edu

University of Arkansas
Fayetteville, AR
uark.edu

California
Academy Pacific Travel College
Hollywood, CA
academypacific.com

Alliant International University
San Diego, CA
alliant.edu

Butte Community College
Oroville, CA
butte.cc.ca.us

California State Polytechnic
University, Pomona
Pomona, CA
csupomona.edu/~cshm

California State University, Chico
Chico, CA
csuchico.edu

California State University, Long
Beach
Long Beach, CA
csulb.edu

California State University,
   Northridge
Northridge, CA
csun.edu

City College of San Francisco
San Francisco, CA
ccsf.edu

Cypress College
Cypress, CA
cypresscollege.org/votech/htc/ind
   ex.htm

Empire Business College
Santa Rosa, CA
empcol.com

Foothill College
Los Altos Hills, CA
bss.foothill.fhda.edu/tc

Global Travel Academy
Sacramento, CA
globaltrav.com

Go Western Travel School
Campbell, CA
gowesterntravelschool.com

International Tour Management
   Institute
San Francisco, CA
itmitourtraining.com

Long Beach City College
Long Beach, CA
lbcc.cc.ca.us

Los Medanos College
Pittsburg, CA
centram.org

Loyola Marymount University
Los Angeles, CA
lmu.edu

Miracosta College
Oceanside, CA
miracosta.edu/travel/default.htm

Mission College
Santa Clara, CA
missioncollege.org

Mount San Antonio College
Walnut, CA
mtsac.edu

Palomar College
San Marcos, CA
palomar.edu

Pomona College
Claremont, CA
pomona.edu

San Bernardino Valley College
San Bernardino, CA
sbvc.sbccd.cc.ca.us

San Diego Mesa College
San Diego, CA
sdmesa.sdccd.net

San Diego State University
San Diego, CA
sdsu.edu

San Francisco State University
San Francisco, CA
sfsu.edu

Santa Barbara City College
Santa Barbara, CA
sbcc.cc.ca.us

Santa Monica College
Santa Monica, CA
smc.edu/bus

Santiago Canyon College
Orange, CA
sccollege.edu

Travel Experts School
San Diego, CA
travelschool.org

Travel University
San Diego, CA
traveluniversity.edu

Trav-l-world Agency & College
Los Angeles, CA
trav-l-world.com

Tri-Cities Regional Occupation
   Program
Whittier, CA
tcrop.k12.ca.us

University of California, Irvine
Irvine, CA
uci.edu

University of San Francisco
San Francisco, CA
usfca.edu

West Coast School of Travel
Woodland Hills, CA
wctravelschool.com

West Los Angeles College
Culver City, CA
wlac.cc.us/travel

Colorado
Arapahoe Community College
Littleton, CO
arapahoe.edu

Colorado State University
Fort Collins, CO
colostate.edu

Fort Lewis College
Durango, CO
fortlewis.edu

International Guide Academy
Boulder, CO
igaonline.com

Mesa State College/UTEC
Grand Junction, CO
mesastate.edu

Metropolitan State College
Denver, CO
mscd.edu

Northeastern Junior College
Sterling, CO
njc.edu

Parks Junior College
Denver, CO
parks-college.com

University of Colorado at Boulder
Boulder, CO
colorado.edu

University of Denver
Denver, CO
dcb.du.edu

Connecticut
American Educational Institute
Bridgeport, CT
gotrain.com/schools/112.htm

Briarwood College
Southington, CT
briarwood.edu

Central Connecticut State
    University
New Britain, CT
ccsu.edu

Gateway Community College
New Haven, CT
gwctc.commnet.edu

Grasso Southeastern RVTS
Groton, CT
cttech.org/grasso/index.htm

International College of
    Hospitality Management
Washington, CT
ichm.ritz.edu

Naugatuck Valley Community
    Technical College
Waterbury, CT
nvcc.commnet.edu

Norwalk Community College
Norwalk, CT
nctc.commnet.edu

Stone Academy
Hamden, CT
stoneacademy.com

Teikyo Post University
Waterbury, CT
teikyopost.edu

University of New Haven
West Haven, CT
newhaven.edu/tourism

Delaware
Delaware State University
Dover, DE
dsc.edu

Delaware Technical &
    Community College
Georgetown, DE
dtcc.edu

Tech Prep Delaware
Dover, DE
techprepdelaware.org

University of Delaware
Newark, DE
udel.edu/hrim

Florida

Bethune-Cookman College
Daytona Beach, FL
bethune.cookman.edu

Broward Community College
Fort Lauderdale, FL
broward.edu

Central Florida Community
College
Ocala, FL
gocfcc.com

Daytona Beach Community
College
Daytona Beach, FL
dbcc.cc.fl.us

Educational Institute of the
American Hotel and Lodging
Association
Orlando, FL
ei-ahla.org

First Coast Technical Institute
Saint Augustine, FL
fcti.org

Florida Atlantic University
Boca Raton, FL
fau.edu

Florida Community College at
Jacksonville
Jacksonville, FL
fccj.org

Florida Culinary Institute
West Palm Beach, FL
floridaculinary.com

Florida International University
North Miami, FL
hospitality.fiu.edu

Florida National College
Hialeah, FL
fnc.edu

Florida State University
Tallahassee, FL
cob.fsu.edu/ha

Gulf Coast Community College
Panama City, FL
gc.cc.fl.us

Johnson and Wales University
North Miami, FL
jwu.edu/florida/index.htm

Keiser College
Fort Lauderdale, FL
keisercollege.cc.fl.us

Lynn University
Boca Raton, FL
lynn.edu

Manatee Technical College
Bradenton, FL
manateetechnicalinstitute.org

Miami Dade College
Miami, FL
mdcc.edu

Miami-Dade Community
   College–Wolfson Campus
Miami, FL
mdcc.edu

Mid Florida Tech
Orlando, FL
mft.ocps.net/travtour.htm

Nova Southeastern University
Fort Lauderdale, FL
nova.edu

Palm Beach Community College
Lake Worth, FL
pbcc.cc.fl.us

Pensacola Junior College
Pensacola, FL
pjc.cc.fl.us

Saint Thomas University
Miami, FL
stu.edu

Schiller International University
Dunedin, FL
schiller.edu

Seminole Community College
Sanford, FL
scc-fl.edu

Sheridan Vo-Tech Center
Hollywood, FL
scc-fl.edu

South Florida Travel Academy
Miami Lakes, FL
travinst.com/sfta

Travel Career Institute
Boca Raton, FL
travelschool.net/index.htm

University of Central Florida
Orlando, FL
hospitality.ucf.edu

Valencia Community College
Orlando, FL
valencia.cc.fl.us

Webber International University
Babson Park, FL
webber.edu

Webster College
Tampa, FL
webstercollege.com

Georgia

Georgia Southern University
Statesboro, GA
gasou.edu

Georgia State University
Atlanta, GA
robinson.gsu.edu/hospitality

Morris Brown College
Atlanta, GA
morrisbrown.edu

Savannah State College
Savannah, GA
savstate.edu

Hawaii

Brigham Young
   University–Hawaii
Laie, HI
byuh.edu

Hawaii Pacific University
Honolulu, HI
hpu.edu

Kapiolani Community College
Honolulu, HI
kcc.hawaii.edu

Travel Institute of the Pacific
Honolulu, HI
tiphawaii.com

Travel University International
Honolulu, HI
traveluniversity.edu

University of Hawaii at Manoa
Honolulu, HI
tim.hawaii.edu

Idaho

The College of Southern Idaho
Twin Falls, ID
csi.edu

North Idaho College
Coeur d'Alene, ID
northidahocollege.edu

University of Idaho
Moscow, ID
cnr.uidaho.edu/rrt

Illinois

Belleville Area College
Granite City, IL
southwestern.cc.il.us/belleville

Black Hawk College
East Moline, IL
bhc.edu/bcec/travel/curriculum
   .htm

Bradley University
Peoria, IL
bradley.edu

Chicago State University
Chicago, IL
csu.edu

College of Dupage
Glen Ellyn, IL
cod.edu

Elgin Community College
Elgin, IL
elgin.edu

Joliet Junior College
Joliet, IL
jjc.cc.il.us

Kendall College
Chicago, IL
kendall.edu

Lexington College
Chicago, IL
lexingtoncollege.edu

Lincoln College
Normal, IL
lincolncollege.edu/normal

Lincoln Land Community College
Springfield, IL
llcc.cc.il.us

Moraine Valley Community
College
Palos Hills, IL
morainevalley.edu

Northern Illinois University
Dekalb, IL
niu.edu

Northwestern Business College
Chicago, IL
northwesternbc.edu

Northwestern University
Evanston, IL
northwestern.edu

Parkland College
Champaign, IL
parkland.cc.il.us

Robert Morris College
Chicago, IL
robertmorris.edu

Roosevelt University
Chicago, IL
roosevelt.edu

Southern Illinois University at
Carbondale
Carbondale, IL
siu.edu

Triton College
Arlington Heights, IL
triton.edu

University of Illinois at
Urbana–Champaign
Champaign, IL
uiuc.edu

Western Illinois University
Macomb, IL
wiu.edu/users/mirpta

William Rainey Harper College
Palatine, IL
harpercollege.edu

Indiana

Ambassador Institute of Travel
Evansville, IN
ambassadorcruise.com

Ball State University
Muncie, IN
bsu.edu/geog

Indiana Travel Academy
Fort Wayne, IN
edgertonstravel.com/career.asp

Indiana University at
    Bloomington
Bloomington, IN
indiana.edu/~recpark

Indiana University–Purdue
    University Fort Wayne
Fort Wayne, IN
ipfw.edu

Indiana University–Purdue
    University Indianapolis
Indianapolis, IN
iupui.edu/~indyhper

Indiana Vocational Technical
    College
Hammond, IN
lowell.net/chamber/educate.htm

International Business College
Fort Wayne, IN
design-training.com/bc-
    ftwayne.mail.html

Ivy Tech State College
Indianapolis, IN
ivytech.edu/indianapolis

Purdue University
West Lafayette, IN
cfs.purdue.edu/htm

University of Southern Indiana
Evansville, IN
usi.edu

Iowa

AIB College of Business
Des Moines, IA
aib.edu

Cedar Falls–Hamilton College
Cedar Falls, IA
hamiltonia.edu

Davenport–Kaplan College
Davenport, IA
kaplancollegeia.com

Hamilton College
Mason City, IA
hamiltonia.edu

Iowa Lakes Community College
Emmetsburg, IA
iowalakes.edu

Iowa State University
Ames, IA
fcs.iastate.edu/hrim

Iowa Western Community
   College
Council Bluffs, IA
iwcc.edu

Kirkwood Community College
Cedar Rapids, IA
kirkwoodcollege.com

Kansas
Bryan College
Topeka, KS
bryancollege.com

Johnson County Community
   College
Overland Park, KS
jccc.net

Kansas State University
Manhattan, KS
humec.ksu.edu

Kentucky
Eastern Kentucky University
Richmond, KY
eku.edu

Morehead State University
Morehead, KY
moreheadstate.edu

Sullivan University–Lexington
Lexington, KY
sullivan.edu/lexington

Sullivan University–Louisville
Louisville, KY
sullivan.edu/louisville

Transylvania University
Lexington, KY
transylvaniauniversity.edu

University of Kentucky
Lexington, KY
uky.edu

Western Kentucky University
Bowling Green, KY
wku.edu/hospitality

Louisiana
Delgado Community College
New Orleans, LA
dcc.edu

Grambling State University
Grambling, LA
gram.edu

Tulane University
New Orleans, LA
tulane.edu

University of Louisiana at
   Lafayette
Lafayette, LA
louisiana.edu

University of New Orleans
New Orleans, LA
uno.edu

Maine

Andover College
Portland, ME
andovercollege.com

Beal College
Bangor, ME
bealcollege.org

Husson College
Bangor, ME
husson.edu

University of Maine
Orono, ME
umaine.edu

York County Technical College
Wells, ME
yctc.net

Maryland

Anne Arundel Community
   College
Arnold, MD
www.aacc.cc.md.us

Baltimore City Community
   College
Baltimore, MD
culinaryschools.com/schools

Baltimore's International
   Culinary College
Baltimore, MD
bic.edu

Chesapeake College
Wye Mills, MD
chesapeake.edu

Essex Community College
Baltimore County, MD
ccbc.cc.md.us

Montgomery College
Rockville, MD
montgomerycollege.edu

Morgan State University
Baltimore, MD
morgan.edu

University of Maryland–
   Eastern Shore
Princess Anne, MD
umes.edu

Villa Julie College
Stevenson, MD
vjc.edu

Massachusetts

Bay State College
Boston, MA
baystate.edu

Becker College
Worcester, MA
beckercollege.edu

Boston University
Boston, MA
bu.edu

Cape Cod Community College
West Barnstable, MA
capecod.mass.edu

Framingham State College
Framingham, MA
framingham.edu

Holyoke Community College
Holyoke, MA
hcc.mass.edu/html

Lasell College
Newton, MA
lasell.edu

Massachusetts Bay Community
College
Wellesley, MA
mbcc.mass.edu

Massasoit Community College
Brockton, MA
massasoit.mass.edu

Middlesex Community College
Lowell, MA
middlesex.mass.edu

Newbury College
Brookline, MA
newbury.edu

Northeastern University
Boston, MA
northeastern.edu

Quinsigamond Community
College
Worcester, MA
qcc.mass.edu

Salem State College
Salem, MA
salemstate.edu

University of Massachusetts,
Amherst
Amherst, MA
umass.edu

Westfield State College
Westfield, MA
wsc.mass.edu

Michigan
Avanti Travel School
Fenton, MI
seashoreair.com

Central Michigan University
Mount Pleasant, MI
cmich.cdu

Conlin-Hallissey Travel School
Ann Arbor, MI
travelstudent.com

Eastern Michigan University
Ypsilanti, MI
emich.edu

Educational Institute of the
American Hotel & Lodging
Association
East Lansing, MI
ei-ahla.org

Ferris State University
Big Rapids, MI
ferris.edu/hospitality

Grand Rapids Community
College
Grand Rapids, MI
grcc.cc.mi.us

Grand Valley State University
Allendale, MI
gvsu.edu

Henry Ford Community College
Dearborn, MI
hfcc.net

Jackson Community College
Jackson, MI
jackson.cc.mi.us

Lansing Community College
Lansing, MI
lcc.edu

Livonia Career Technical Center
Livonia, MI
www.livonia.k12.mi.us/schools/
high/center

Michigan State University
East Lansing, MI
bus.msu.edu

Mott Community College
Flint, MI
mcc.edu

Northern Michigan University
Marquette, MI
nmu.edu

Northwestern Michigan College
Traverse City, MI
nmc.edu

Northwood University
Midland, MI
northwood.edu

Oakland Community College
Farmington Hills, MI
occ.cc.mi.us

Sienna Heights College
Adrian, MI
sienahts.edu

Suomi College
Hancock, MI
suomi.edu

Travel Education Institute–Grand
Rapids Campus
Grand Rapids, MI
travinst.com

Travel Education
  Institute–Southfield Campus
Southfield, MI
travinst.com

Western Michigan University
Kalamazoo, MI
wmich.edu

Minnesota

Alexandria Technical College
Alexandria, MN
alextech.org

Art Institutes International
  Minnesota
Minneapolis, MN
aim.artinstitutes.edu

Central Lakes College
Brainerd, MN
clc.mnscu.edu

Dakota County Technical College
Rosemount, MN
dctc.edu

The McConnell School, Inc.
Minneapolis, MN
mcconnellschool.com

Minneapolis Business College
Roseville, MN
minneapolisbusinesscollege.edu

Normandale Community College
Bloomington, MN
normandale.edu

Rasmussen Business College
Minnetonka, MN
rasmussen.edu

Riverland Community College
Albert Lea, MN
riverland.edu

Saint Cloud State University
Saint Cloud, MN
stcloudstate.edu

Southwest Minnesota State
  University
Marshall, MN
southwest.msus.edu

University of
  Minnesota–Crookston
Crookston, MN
crk.umn.edu

Mississippi

University of Mississippi
University, MS
olemiss.edu

University of Southern
  Mississippi
Hattiesburg, MS
usm.edu

Missouri

Central Missouri State University
Warrensburg, MO
cmsu.edu

Maple Woods Community
College
Kansas City, MO
kcmetro.edu

Patricia Stevens College
Saint Louis, MO
patriciastevenscollege.com

Penn Valley Community College
Kansas City, MO
kcmetro.edu

Saint Louis Community College
at Forest Park
Saint Louis, MO
stlcc.edu

Southwest Missouri State
University
Springfield, MO
smsu.edu

University of Missouri–Columbia
Columbia, MO
fse.missouri.edu/hrm

Montana
Flathead Valley Community
College
Kalispell, MT
fucc.cc.mt.us

University of Montana
Missoula, MT
umt.edu

Nebraska
Central Community College
Hastings, NE
cccneb.edu

Hamilton College
Lincoln, NE
lincolnschoolofcommerce.com

Hamilton College–Omaha
Omaha, NE
ncbedu.com

Metropolitan Community College
Omaha, NE
mccneb.edu

Southeast Community College
Lincoln, NE
southeast.edu

Travel Careers Institute
Omaha, NE
tandt.com

Nevada
Community College of Southern
Nevada
North Las Vegas, NV
ccsn.nevada.edu

Las Vegas–Heritage College
Las Vegas, NV
heritagecollege.com

Sierra Nevada College–
   Lake Tahoe
Incline Village, NV
sierranevada.edu

University of Nevada, Las Vegas
Las Vegas, NV
unlv.edu

University of Nevada, Reno
Reno, NV
unr.edu

New Hampshire

Hesser College
Manchester, NH
hesser.edu

New Hampshire Technical
   Institute
Concord, NH
nhti.net

New Hampshire Vocational
   Technical College
Berlin, NH
berlin.nhctc.edu

Plymouth State College
Plymouth, NH
plymouth.edu

University of New Hampshire
Durham, NH
orbit.unh.edu/dhm

New Jersey

Atlantic Cape Community
   College
Mays Landing, NJ
atlantic.edu

Bergen Community College
Paramus, NJ
bergen.edu

Berkeley College
West Paterson, NJ
collegesinnewjersey.com

County College of Morris
Randolph, NJ
ccm.edu

Fairleigh Dickinson University
Teaneck, NJ
fdu.edu

Georgian Court College
Lakewood, NJ
georgiancourtcollege.edu

Hudson Valley Community
   College
Jersey City, NJ
hudson.cc.nj.us

Mercer County Community
   College
Trenton, NJ
mccc.edu

Middlesex County College
Edison, NJ
middlesexcc.edu

Montclair State University
Upper Montclair, NJ
montclair.edu

Richard Stockton College
Pomona, NJ
stockton.edu

New Mexico
Dona Ana Branch Community
  College
Las Cruces, NM
dabcc-nmsu.edu

New Mexico Highlands University
Las Vegas, NM
nmhu.edu

New Mexico State University
Las Cruces, NM
nmsu.edu/~hrtm

University of New Mexico
Albuquerque, NM
traveltourism.mgt.unm.edu

New York
Adirondack Community College
Queensbury, NY
sunyacc.edu

American Institute of Tourism
New York, NY
nit-ait.com

Baruch College
New York, NY
baruch.cuny.edu

Borough of Manhattan
  Community College
New York City, NY
bmcc.cuny.edu

Bryant & Stratton Business
  Institute
Syracuse, NY
bryantstratton.edu

Buffalo State College
Buffalo, NY
buffalostate.edu

Buffalo State University
Buffalo, NY
buffalo.edu

Cornell University
Ithaca, NY
cornell.edu

Erie Community College North
Williamsville, NY
ecu.edu

Finger Lakes Community College
Canandaigua, NY
fingerlakes.edu

Genesee Community College
Batavia, NY
genesee.edu

Herkimer County Community
  College
Herkimer, NY
hccc.suny.edu

Jefferson Community College
Watertown, NY
sunyjefferson.edu

Keuka College
New York, NY
univsource.com/ny.htm

Kingsborough Community
  College
Brooklyn, NY
kbcc.cuny.edu

LaGuardia Community
  College
Long Island City, NY
lagcc.cuny.edu

Mercy College
Dobbs Ferry, NY
mercy.edu

Mohawk Valley Community
  College
Rome, NY
mvcc.edu

Monroe Community College
Rochester, NY
monroecc.edu

Morrisville State College
Morrisville, NY
morrisville.edu

Nassau Community College
Garden City, NY
ncc.edu

New York Institute of Technology
Central Islip, NY
nyit.edu

New York University
New York, NY
scps.nyu.edu/tischcenter

Niagara County Community
  College
Sanborn, NY
niagaracc.suny.edu

Niagara University
Niagara University, NY
niagara.edu/hospitality

Pace University
New York, NY
pace.edu

Paul Smith's College of Arts &
  Science
Paul Smiths, NY
paulsmiths.edu

Ridley-Lowell Business &
  Technology Institute
Binghamton, NY
ridley.edu

Rochester Institute of Technology
Rochester, NY
rit.edu

Rockland Community College
Suffern, NY
sunyrockland.edu

Saint Johns University
Jamaica, NY
stjohns.edu

Schenectady County Community
College
Schenectady, NY
sunysccc.edu

State University of New York
Agricultural Technical College
Canton, NY
univsource.com/ny.htm

State University of New York at
Cobleskill
Cobleskill, NY
cobleskill.edu

State University of New York at
Oneonta
Oneonta, NY
oneonta.edu

State University of New York at
Delhi
Delhi, NY
delhi.edu

Sullivan County Community
College
Loch Sheldrake, NY
sullivan.suny.edu

Syracuse University
Syracuse, NY
syr.edu

North Carolina
Appalachian State University
Boone, NC
appstate.edu

Asheville-Buncombe Technical
Community College
Asheville, NC
abtech.edu

Barber Scotia College
Concord, NC
b-sc.edu

Blue Ridge Community College
Flat Rock, NC
blueridge.cc.nc.us

Cape Fear Community College
Wilmington, NC
cfcc.edu

Central Piedmont Community
College
Charlotte, NC
cpcc.edu

East Carolina University
Greenville, NC
ecu.edu/hes/nuhm/nuhmhome
.htm

North Carolina Central
University
Durham, NC
nccu.edu

North Carolina State University
Raleigh, NC
ncsu.edu

North Carolina Wesleyan College
Rocky Mount, NC
ncwc.edu

Southwestern Community
College
Sylva, NC
southwest.cc.nc.us

University of North Carolina
Chapel Hill, NC
unc.edu

University of North Carolina at
Greensboro
Greensboro, NC
uncg.edu/rpt

University of North Carolina at
Wilmington
Wilmington, NC
uncwil.edu/hahs

Wake Technical Community
College
Raleigh, NC
waketech.nc.us

Western Carolina University
Cullowhee, NC
wcu.edu

Wilkes Community College
Wilkesboro, NC
wilkescc.edu

North Dakota
North Dakota State University
Fargo, ND
ndsu.nodak.edu

Ohio
Bowling Green State University
Bowling Green, OH
bgsu.edu

Central State University
Wilberforce, OH
centralstate.edu

Columbus State Community
College
Columbus, OH
cscc.edu

Cuyahoga Community College
Cleveland, OH
tri-c.edu

Kent State University
Kent, OH
kent.edu

Lakeland Community College
Kirtland, OH
lakeland.cc.oh.us

Ohio State University
Athens, OH
hhs.ohiou.edu/index.asp

Ohio University Southern
Campus
Ironton, OH
southern.ohiou.edu

Sinclair Community College
Dayton, OH
sinclair.edu

Tiffin University
Tiffin, OH
tiffin.edu

Tri-State Travel School
Cincinnati, OH
travelcareers.com

Oklahoma
Northeastern State University
Tahlequah, OK
arapaho.nsuok.edu/~mdm

Oklahoma State University
Stillwater, OK
osuhrad.org

Oregon
Central Oregon Community
College
Bend, OR
cocc.edu

Chemeketa Community College
Salem, OR
hsm.org

Mount Hood Community College
Gresham, OR
mhcc.edu

Oregon State University
Corvallis, OR
oregonstate.edu

Portland Community College
Portland, OR
pcc.edu

Southern Oregon University
Ashland, OR
sou.edu

Western Culinary Institute
Portland, OR
wci.edu

Pennsylvania
Bucks County Community
College
Newtown, PA
bucks.edu

California University of
    Pennsylvania
California, PA
cup.edu

Central Pennsylvania College
Summerdale, PA
centralpenn.edu

Delaware County Community
    College
Media, PA
dccc.edu

Drexel University
Philadelphia, PA
drexel.edu

East Stroudsburg University
East Stroudsburg, PA
esu.edu

Education Direct
Scranton, PA
educationdircct.com

Harcum College
Bryn Mawr, PA
harcum.edu

Harrisburg Area Community
    College
Harrisburg, PA
hacc.edu

The Hospitality Training Institute
Philadelphia, PA
philaoic.org

ICM School of Business
Pittsburgh, PA
icmschool.com

Indiana University of
    Pennsylvania
Indiana, PA
iup.edu/hr

Keystone Junior College
La Plume, PA
keystone.edu

Lehigh Carbon Community
    College
Allentown, PA
lccc.edu

Luzerne County Community
    College
Nanticoke, PA
luzerne.edu

Mansfield University
Mansfield, PA
mnsfld.cdu

Marywood University
Scranton, PA
marywood.edu

Mercyhurst College
Erie, PA
mercyhurst.edu

Pennsylvania College of
Technology
Williamsport, PA
pct.edu

Pennsylvania State University
University Park, PA
psu.edu

Reading Area Community College
Reading, PA
racc.edu

Robert Morris College
Corapolis, PA
robert-morris.edu

Temple University
Philadelphia, PA
temple.edu/sthm

Westmoreland County
Community College
Youngwood, PA
wccc-pa.edu

Widener University
Chester, PA
widener.edu/hospitality/sohm
.html

York Technical Institute
York, PA
yti.edu

Rhode Island
Johnson & Wales University
Providence, RI
jwu.edu

University of Rhode Island
Kingston, RI
uri.edu

South Carolina
Clemson University
Clemson, SC
clemson.edu

Coastal Carolina University
Conway, SC
coastal.edu

College of Charleston
Charleston, SC
cofc.edu/~baecon/tourism.htm

Horry Georgetown Technical
College
Myrtle Beach, SC
hor.tec.sc.us/hospitality

Johnson & Wales
University–Charleston
Charleston, SC
jwu.edu/charleston

Technical College of the
Lowcountry
Beaufort, SC
tcl-tec-sc-us.org

Trident Technical College
Charleston, SC
tridenttech.edu

University of South Carolina
Columbia, SC
hrsm.sc.edu

Winthrop College
Rock Hill, SC
winthrop.edu

South Dakota

Black Hills State University
Spearfish, SD
bhsu.edu

National College
Rapid City, SD
national.edu

South Dakota State University
Brookings, SD
sdstate.edu

Tennessee

Belmont University
Nashville, TN
belmont.edu

Kemmons Wilson School of
   Hospitality & Resort
   Management
Memphis, TN
wilson.memphis.edu

Southwest Tennessee Community
   College
Memphis, TN
southwest.tn.edu

University of Memphis
Memphis, TN
memphis.edu/hospitality

University of Tennessee
Knoxville, TN
utk.edu

Volunteer State Community
   College
Gallatin, TN
volstate.edu

Texas

Austin Community College
Austin, TX
austincc.edu

Capitol City Careers
Austin, TX
capcitycareers.com

Collin County Community
   College
Frisco, TX
ccccd.edu/hospitality

Conrad Hilton College of Hotel &
   Restaurant Management
Houston, TX
hrm.uh.edu

Del Mar College
Corpus Christi, TX
delmar.edu

El Paso Community College
El Paso, TX
epcc.edu

Houston Community College
Houston, TX
hccs.cc.tx.us

North Harris County College
Kingwood, TX
nhmccd.edu

Richland College
Dallas, TX
rlc.dcccd.edu/travel/index.htm

Saint Philip's Community College
San Antonio, TX
accd.edu/spc

Southern Methodist University
Dallas, TX
smu.edu

Tarrant County
  College–Southeast
Arlington, TX
tccd.edu

Texas A & M University
College Station, TX
tamu.edu

Texas State Technical
  College–Waco
Waco, TX
waco.tstc.edu

Texas Tech University
Lubbock, TX
ttacs.ttu.edu

University of Houston
Houston, TX
uh.edu

University of North Texas
Denton, TX
smhm.unt.edu

University of Texas at San
  Antonio
San Antonio, TX
utsa.edu

Wiley College
Marshall, TX
wileyc.edu

Utah
Brigham Young University
Provo, UT
byu.edu

Education Systems
Sandy, UT
educationsystems.com

Mountain West College
West Valley City, UT
mountainwest.edu

University of Utah
Salt Lake City, UT
utah.edu

Utah Valley State College
Orem, UT
uvsc.edu

Vermont

Champlain College
Burlington, VT
champlain.edu/majors/hospitality
/index.php

Johnson State College
Johnson, VT
jsc.vsc.edu/htm

University of Vermont
Burlington, VT
uvm.edu

Virginia

College of William & Mary
Williamsburg, VA
wm.edu

Commonwealth College
Virginia Beach, VA
vcu.edu

George Mason University
Manassas, VA
gmu.edu

J. Sargeant Reynolds Community
College
Richmond, VA
jsr.vccs.edu

James Madison University
Harrisonburg, VA
jmu.edu

Norfolk State University
Norfolk, VA
nsu.edu

Northern Virginia Community
College
Annandale, VA
nvcc.edu

Omega Travel School
Fairfax, VA
owt.net

Tidewater Community College
Virginia Beach, VA
tc.cc.va.us

Virginia Polytechnic Institute and
State University
Blacksburg, VA
vt.edu

Virginia State University
Petersburg, VA
vsu.edu

Washington

Bates Technical College
Lakewood, WA
bates.ctc.edu

Bellingham Technical College
Bellingham, WA
beltc.ctc.edu

Central Washington University
Ellensburg, WA
cwu.edu

Clover Park Technical College
Tacoma, WA
cptc.ctc.edu

Fox Travel Institute
Seattle, WA
davethefox.com

International Air Academy, Inc.
Vancouver, WA
airacademy.com

Seattle Central Community
    College
Seattle, WA
seattlecentral.org

Spokane Community College
Spokane, WA
ccs.spokane.cc.wa.us

University of Washington
Seattle, WA
washington.edu

Washington State University
Pullman, WA
cbe.wsu.edu/hbm/index.html

Washington, D.C.

George Washington University
Washington, DC
gwutourism.org

Howard University
Washington, DC
howard.edu

West Virginia

Concord College
Athens, WV
concord.wvnet.edu

Davis & Elkins College
Elkins, WV
davisandelkins.edu

Fairmont State Community &
    Technical College
Fairmont, WV
fscwv.edu

West Liberty State College
West Liberty, WV
wlsc.edu

West Virginia State College
Institute, WV
wvsc.edu

Wisconsin

Adelman Travel Academy
Milwaukee, WI
learntravel.com

Gateway Technical College
Kenosha, WI
gateway.tec.wi.us

Madison Area Technical College
Madison, WI
matcmadison.edu

Milwaukee Area Technical College
Milwaukee, WI
milwaukee.tec.wi.us

Moraine Park Technical College
Fond du Lac, WI
moraine.tec.wi.us

Nicolet Area Technical College
Rhinelander, WI
nicoletcollege.edu

University of Wisconsin
Kenosha, WI
uwp.edu

University of Wisconsin–Eau
   Claire
Eau Claire, WI
uwec.edu

University of Wisconsin–Stout
Menomonie, WI
uwstout.edu

Waukesha County Technical
   College
Pewaukee, WI
wctc.edu

Wyoming

Casper College
Casper, WY
caspercollege.edu

Northwest College
Powell, WY
northwestcollege.org

Sheridan College
Sheridan, WY
sc.ec.wy.us

CANADA

Alberta
Southern Alberta Institute of
   Technology
Calgary, AB
sait.ab.ca/flash.htm

British Columbia
Camosun College
Victoria, BC
camosun.bc.ca

Canadian Tourism College–Surrey
Surrey, BC
tourismcollege.com

Canadian Tourism
   College–Vancouver
Vancouver, BC
tourismcollege.com

University College of the Cariboo
Kamloops, BC
cariboo.bc.ca

University of Victoria
Victoria, BC
business.uvic.ca

Manitoba
Assiniboine Community College
Brandon, MB
assiniboine.net

Red River College
Winnipeg, MB
rrc.mb.ca

New Brunswick
University of New Brunswick
Saint John, NB
business.unbsj.ca

Nova Scotia
Mount Saint Vincent University
Halifax, NS
msvu.ca

Ontario
Algonquin College
Ottawa, ON
algonquincollege.com/hospitality

Brock University
Saint Catherines, ON
brocku.ca/tourism

Centennial College
Scarborough, ON
centennialcollege.ca

Fanshawe College
London, ON
fanshawec.ca

Humber College
Toronto, ON
humberc.on.ca

Lambton College
Sarnia, ON
lambton.on.ca

Niagara College Canada
Niagara-on-the-Lake, ON
niagarac.on.ca

Ryerson University
Toronto, ON
ryerson.ca/shtm

Saint Clair College
Windsor, ON
stclaircollege.ca

Seneca College
King City, ON
senecac.on.ca

Sir Sandford Fleming College
Peterborough, ON
flemingc.on.ca

University of Guelph
Guelph, ON
uoguelph.ca

University of Waterloo
Waterloo, ON
ahs.uwaterloo.ca

Prince Edward Island
Holland College
Charlottetown, PE
hollandc.pe.ca

Quebec
Champlain Regional College
Saint Lambert, QC
champlaincollege.qc.ca

College of Granby
    Haute–Yamaska
Granby, QC
cegepgranby.qc.ca

Concordia University
Montreal, QC
concordia.ca

Institute of Tourism and Hotels
    of Quebec
Montreal, QC
ithq.qc.ca

University of Quebec at
    Montreal–ESG
Montreal, QC
esg.uqam.ca

APPENDIX D

POST-SECONDARY SCHOOLS WITH RESTAURANT AND FOOD-SERVICE PROGRAMS

The following list of postsecondary restaurant and food-service programs in the United States is provided by the National Restaurant Association Educational Foundation (NRAEF).

Alabama
Culinard: The Culinary Institute
    of Virginia College
Birmingham, AL
culinard.com

Alaska
Alaska Vocational Technical
    Center
Seward, AK
avtec.labor.state.ak.us

Arizona
Central Arizona College
Coolidge, AZ
cac.cc.az.us

Northland Pioneer College
Holbrook, AZ
northland.cc.az.us

Pima Community College
Tucson, AZ
pima.edu

Arkansas
ACF/Central Arkansas Chapter
    Culinary School of
    Apprenticeship
Little Rock, AR
acfchefs.org

North Arkansas Community &
    Technical College
Harrison, AR
northark.edu

Ouachita Technical College
Malvern, AR
otcweb.org

California

Allan Hancock Community
  College
Santa Maria, CA
hancock.cc.ca.us

American River College
Sacramento, CA
arc.losrios.edu

Art Institute of California–San
  Diego
San Diego, CA
allartschools.com

Bakersfield College
Bakersfield, CA
bakersfieldcollege.edu

California Culinary Academy
San Francisco, CA
baychef.com

California Department of
  Rehabilitation
San Diego, CA
rehab.cahwnet.gov

California State University–Long
  Beach
Long Beach, CA
csulb.edu

College of the Canyons
Santa Clarita, CA
coc.cc.ca.us

Cosumnes River College
Sacramento, CA
crc.losrios.edu

Cypress College
Cypress, CA
cypress.cc.ca.us

Fresno City College
Fresno, CA
fresnocitycollege.com

Grossmont Community College
Fresno, CA
gcccd.cc.ca.us

Institute of Culinary Arts
Fresno, CA
foodsupplier.com/culinaryschools

Los Angeles Mission College
Sylmar, CA
lamission.edu

Mira Costa College
Oceanside, CA
miracosta.cc.ca.us

Mission College
Santa Clara, CA
missioncollege.org

Oxnard College
Oxnard, CA
oxnardcollege.edu

San Diego Community College
  Auxiliary Organization
San Diego, CA
sdicregionalconsortium.org/
  coned.html

Shasta College
Redding, CA
shastacollege.edu

Southern California School of
  Culinary Arts
South Pasadena, CA
scsca.com

Victor Valley Community College
Victorville, CA
victor.cc.ca.us

Colorado
Arapahoe Community College
Littleton, CO
arapahoe.edu

Front Range Community
  College–Lorimer
Fort Collins, CO
coloradomentor.org

Mesa State College/UTEC
Grand Junction, CO
mesastate.edu

Pikes Peak Community College
Colorado Springs, CO
ppcc.cccoes.edu

Pueblo Community College
Pueblo, CO
pueblocc.edu

Connecticut
Gateway Community-Technical
  College
New Haven, CT
gwctc.commnet.edu

Manchester Community-
  Technical College
Manchester, CT
universities.com/schools/m/
  manchester_community_
  technical_college.asp

Norwalk Community-Technical
  College
Norwalk, CT
nctc.commnet.edu

Delaware
Delaware State University
Dover, DE
desu.edu

Delaware Technical &
  Community College–Stanton
  Campus
Newark, DE
dtcc.edu/owens

Florida
Bethune Cookman College
Daytona Beach, FL
bethune.cookman.edu

Florida Community College
Jacksonville, FL
fccj.org

Florida Culinary Institute
West Palm Beach, FL
floridaculinary.com

Florida State University
Tallahassee, FL
fsu.edu

Lynn University
Boca Raton, FL
lynn.edu

Orlando Culinary Academy
Orlando, FL
orlandoculinary.com

Pensacola Junior College
Pensacola, FL
pjc.cc.fl.us

Southeast Institute of Culinary
 Arts
Saint Augustine, FL
fcti.org

Webber College
Babson Park, FL
webber.edu

Georgia
Culinary Arts
Augusta, GA
augusta.tec.ga.us

Idaho
Lewis-Clark State College
Lewiston, ID
lcsc.edu

Illinois
Belleville Area College
Granite City, IL
southwestern.cc.il.us

Carl Sandburg College
Galesburg, IL
sandburg.edu

CHIC–Cooking and Hospitality
 Institute of Chicago
Chicago, IL
chic.edu

College of DuPage
Glen Ellyn, IL
cod.edu

Columbia College
Chicago, IL
colum.edu

Elgin Community College
Elgin, IL
elgin.edu

Illinois Central College
East Peoria, IL
icc.edu

John Wood Community College
Quincy, IL
jwcc.edu

Joliet Junior College
Joliet, IL
jjc.cc.il.us

Lincoln Land Community College
Springfield, IL
llcc.cc.il.us

Lincoln Trail College
Robinson, IL
iecc.cc.il.us

Malcolm X College
Chicago, IL
malcolmx.ccc.edu

Moraine Valley Community
College
Palos Hills, IL
morainevalley.edu

Oakton Community College
Des Plaines, IL
oakton.edu

Parkland College
Champaign, IL
parkland.edu

Rend Lake College
Ina, IL
rlc.cc.il.us

Richland Community College
Decatur, IL
richland.edu

William Rainey Harper College
Palatine, IL
harpercollege.edu

Indiana

Indiana University–Purdue
University Fort Wayne
Fort Wayne, IN
ipfw.edu

Ivy Tech College
Fort Wayne, IN
ivytech.edu/fortwayne

Ivy Tech State College
Indianapolis, IN
ivytech.edu/indianapolis

Ivy Tech State College
South Bend, IN
ivytech.edu/southbend

Ivy Tech State College Northwest
Gary, IN
gary.ivytech.edu

Marian College
Indianapolis, IN
marian.edu

Vincennes University
Vincennes, IN
vinu.edu

Iowa

Des Moines Area Community
College
Ankeny, IA
dmacc.cc.ia.us

Iowa Lakes Community College
Emmetsburg, IA
ilcc.cc.ia.us

Kirkwood Community College
Cedar Rapids, IA
kirkwood.cc.ia.us

North Iowa Area Community
College
Mason City, IA
niacc.cc.ia.us

Scott Community College
Bettendorf, IA
eicc.edu/scc

Kansas

Johnson County Community
College
Overland Park, KS
johnco.cc.ks.us

Kentucky

Bowling Green Technical College
Bowling Green, KY
bowlinggreen.kctcs.edu

Sullivan College's National Center
for Hospitality Studies
Louisville, KY
sullivan.edu/louisville/national

Louisiana

Bossier Parish Community
College
Bossier City, LA
bpcc.cc.la.us

Delgado Community College
New Orleans, LA
dcc.edu

Grambling State University
Grambling, LA
gram.edu

Lousiana Technical College–Sidell
Campus
Sidell, LA
lctcs.state.la.us

Louisiana Technical
College–Sidney N. Collier
Campus
New Orleans, LA
theltc.net/sidneyncollier

McNeese State University
Lake Charles, LA
mcneese.edu

Nunez Community College
Chalmette, LA
nunez.edu

Maine

Ellsworth Adult Education
Ellsworth, ME
maineadulted.org/members.html

Midcoast School of Technology
Rockland, ME
midcoast.com/melo/about.html

Washington County Community
  College
Calais, ME
mccs.me.edu/transferwccc.html

York County Technical College
Wells, ME
yccc.edu

Maryland

Anne Arundel Community
  College
Arnold, MD
umuc.edu/locate/arundelmills
  .shtml

Hagerstown Community College
Hospitality Training Program
Hagerstown, MD
hcc.cc.md.us

University of Maryland Eastern
  Shore
Ocean City, MD
umes.edu

Massachusetts

Becker College
Worcester, MA
beckercollege.edu

Newbury College
Brookline, MA
newbury.edu

Michigan

Baker College
Muskegon, MI
baker.edu/visit/muskegon.html

Ferris State University
Big Rapids, MI
ferris.edu

Grand Rapids Community
  College
Grand Rapids, MI
grcc.cc.mi.us

Henry Ford Community College
Dearborn, MI
henryford.cc.mi.us

Lake Michigan College
Benton Harbor, MI
lmc.cc.mi.us

Lansing Community College
Lansing, MI
lansing.cc.mi.us

Macomb Community College
Clinton Township, MI
macomb.edu

Montcalm Community College
Sidney, MI
montcalm.cc.mi.us

Mott Community College
Flint, MI
mcc.edu

Northern Michigan University
Marquette, MI
nmu.edu

Northwestern Michigan College
Traverse City, MI
nmc.edu

Oakland Community College
Farmington Hills, MI
occ.cc.mi.us

Schoolcraft College
Livonia, MI
schoolcraft.cc.mi.us

Siena Heights College
Adrian, MI
sienahts.edu

Washtenaw Community College
Ann Arbor, MI
washtenaw.cc.mi.us

Wayne County Community
    College
Detroit, MI
wcccd.edu

Minnesota
Alexandria Technical College
Alexandria, MN
alextech.edu

The Art Institutes International
    Minnesota
Minneapolis, MN
aim.artinstitutes.edu

Technical Center
Brooklyn Park, MN
hennepintech.edu

South Central Technical College
North Mankato, MN
southcentral.edu

Mississippi
Copiah Lincoln Community
    College
Natchez, MS
colin.edu

Northeast Mississippi Community
    College
Booneville, MS
necc.cc.ms.us

Missouri
East Central College
Union, MO
eastcentral.edu

Saint Louis Community College
    at Forest Park
Saint Louis, MO
stlcc.cc.mo.us

Nebraska
McCook Community College
McCook, NE
mpcca.cc.ne.us/mccook.htm

Southeast Community College
Lincoln, NE
southeast.edu

Nevada

Sierra Nevada College
Incline Village, NV
sierranevada.edu

University of Nevada–Las Vegas
Las Vegas, NV
unlv.edu

New Hampshire

Atlantic Culinary Academy
Dover, NH
atlanticculinary.com

New Hampshire College
Manchester, NH
hampshire.edu

New Jersey

Burlington County College
Pemberton, NJ
bcc.edu

County College of Morris
Randolph, NJ
ccm.edu

Mercer County Community
College
Trenton, NJ
mccc.edu

New York

Broome Community College
Binghamton, NY
sunybroome.edu

Erie Community College
Williamsville, NY
ecc.edu

Fulton Montgomery Community
College
Johnstown, NY
fmcc.suny.edu

Jefferson Community College
Watertown, NY
jcc.kctcs.edu

Mohawk Valley Community
College
Rome, NY
mvcc.edu

New York Restaurant School
New York, NY
culinaryschools.com/schools/317
.html

Schenectady County Community
College
Schenectady, NY
sunysccc.edu

State University of New York at
Cobleskill
Cobleskill, NY
cobleskill.edu

State University of New York
Delhi
Delhi, NY
delhi.edu

Suffolk County Community
    College
Riverhead, NY
sunysuffolk.edu

Sullivan County Community
    College
Loch Sheldrake, NY
sullivan.suny.edu

Westchester Community College
Valhalla, NY
sunywcc.edu

North Carolina

Alamance Community College
Graham, NC
alamance.cc.nc.us

Asheville Buncombe Technical
    Community College
Asheville, NC
abtech.edu

Cape Fear Community College
Wilmington, NC
cfcc.edu

Nash Community College
Rocky Mount, NC
nash.cc.nc.us

North Carolina Central
    University
Durham, NC
nccu.edu

North Carolina Wesleyan College
Rocky Mount, NC
ncwc.edu

Robeson Community College
Lumberton, NC
robeson.cc.nc.us

Sand Hills Community College
Pinehurst, NC
sandhills.cc.nc.us

Wake Technical Community
    College
Raleigh, NC
wake.tec.nc.us

Wilkes Community College
Wilkesboro, NC
wilkescc.edu

Ohio

Cincinnati State College
Cincinnati, OH
cinstate.cc.oh.us

Columbus State Community
    College
Columbus, OH
cscc.edu

Cuyahoga Community College
Cleveland, OH
tri-c.cc.oh.us

Jefferson Community College
Steubenville, OH
jeffersoncc.org

Owens Community College
Toledo, OH
owens.edu

Sinclair Community College
Dayton, OH
sinclair.edu

Oklahoma
Metro Technology Centers
Oklahoma City, OK
metrotech.org

Moore-Norman Vocational
  Technical Center
Norman, OK
mntechnology.com

Oregon
Lane Community College
Eugene, OR
lanecc.edu

Pennsylvania
Bucks County Community
  College
Newtown, PA
bucks.edu

Butler County Community
  College
Butler, PA
bc3.edu/toc

Cambria County Area
  Community College
Johnstown, PA
www.ccacc.cc.pa.us

Central Pennsylvania Business
  School
Summerdale, PA
centralpenn.edu

Community College of Alleghany
  County
Pittsburgh, PA
ccac.edu

Harrisburg Area Community
  College
Harrisburg, PA
hacc.edu

JNA Institute of Culinary Arts
Philadelphia, PA
culinaryarts.com

Lehigh Carbon Community
  College
Allentown, PA
lccc.edu

Luzerne County Community
  College
Nanticoke, PA
luzerne.edu

Pennsylvania College of
  Technology
Williamsport, PA
pct.edu

The Restaurant School
Philadelphia, PA
therestaurantschool.com/
  restaurants.asp

Rosemont College
Rosemont, PA
rosemont.edu

Westmoreland County
   Community College
Youngwood, PA
wccc.pa.edu

York Technical Institute
York, PA
yti.edu

South Carolina
Bob Jones University
Greenville, SC
bju.edu

Greenville Technical College
Greenville, SC
greenvilletech.com

Trident Technical College
Charleston, SC
tridenttech.edu

South Dakota
Mitchell Technical Institute
Mitchell, SD
mti.tec.sd.us

Mount Marty College
Yankton, SD
mtmc.edu

Tennessee
Hiwassee College
Madisonville, TN
hiwassee.edu

Opryland Hotel Culinary Institute
Nashville, TN
gaylordhotels.com/
   gaylordopryland/career/
   culinary/apprenticeship.cfm

Volunteer State Community
   College
Gallatin, TN
vscc.cc.tn.us

Texas
Central Texas College
Killeen, TX
ctcd.cc.tx.us

El Centro College
Dallas, TX
ecc.dcccd.edu

El Paso Community College
El Paso, TX
epcc.edu

Galveston College
Galveston, TX
gc.edu

Le Chef College of Hospitality
   Careers
Austin, TX
lechef.org

Panola College
Jefferson, TX
panola.edu

Saint Phillips College
Hospitality Management
San Antonio, TX
accd.edu

Wiley College
Marshall, TX
wileyc.edu

Utah
Salt Lake Community College
Salt Lake City, UT
slcc.edu

Utah Valley State College
Orem, UT
uvsc.edu

Vermont
North Country Career Center
Newport, VT
northcountryschools.org

Virginia
Northern Virginia Community
   College
Annandale, VA
nv.cc.va.us

Virginia Intermont College
Bristol, VA
vic.edu

Virginia State University
Petersburg, VA
vsu.edu

Washington
Art Institute of Seattle
Seattle, WA
ais.edu

Clover Park Technical College
Lakewood, WA
cptc.edu

Skagit Valley College
Mount Vernon, WA
skagit.edu

West Virginia
Fairmont State College
Fairmont, WV
fscwv.edu

Marshall University Community
   and Technical College
Huntington, WV
wvutech.edu

West Virginia University
Morgantown, WV
wvu.edu

Wisconsin
Chippewa Valley Technical
   College
Eau Claire, WI
cvtc.edu

Fox Valley Technical College
Appleton, WI
foxvalley.tec.wi.us

Madison Area Technical College
Madison, WI
witechcolleges.com/matc

Mid-State Technical College
Wisconsin Rapids, WI
www.midstate.tec.wi.us

Milwaukee Area Technical College
Milwaukee, WI
milwaukee.tec.wi.us

Nicolet Area Technical College
Rhinelander, WI
nicoletcollege.edu

Southwest Wisconsin Technical
   College
Fennimore, WI
swtc.edu

Waukesha County Technical
   College
Pewaukee, WI
wctc.edu

Wyoming
American City University
Cheyenne, WY
americancityuni.edu